GETTING

FROM FIRED

TO

HIRED

GETTING FROM FIRED TO HIRED

BOUNCE BACK FROM LOSING YOUR JOB AND GET YOUR CAREER BACK ON TRACK!

BY MARTIN ELKORT

MACMILLAN·USA

Neither the author nor the publisher assumes any responsibilities for actions taken or not taken by readers of this book. This book is a recommended guide through the process of severing employment, finding another job, and seeking financial security. In all cases, professional advice should be sought on individual situations with regard to employment, legal matters, accounting, or other professional services and matters. The author and publisher have taken care to credit any sources of information used in this book and will welcome any information and corrections, omissions, or credits so that future editions may incorporate them.

All names in anecdotes are pseudonyms.

Copyright © 1997 by Martin Elkort

Macmillan General Reference
A Simon & Schuster Macmillan Company
1633 Broadway
New York, NY 10019-6785

An Arco Book

ARCO and colophon are a registered trademark of Simon & Schuster, Inc.
MACMILLAN and colophon are a registered trademark of Macmillan, Inc.

Manufactured in the United States of America

10 9 8 7 6 5 4 3 2 1

Library of Congress Cataloging-in-Publication Data: 96-079995

ISBN: 0-02-861737-1

This book is dedicated to those wanderers in the purgatory of unemployment.

They had a great job.
They were sheltered, given free food,
all they could eat at any time they wanted,
nothing to do all day except enjoy their workplace.
There was only one company rule:
Stay away from where the knowledge is stored!
When they broke that rule,
Adam and Eve were fired, by God,
from the best job anyone ever had.
The rest is history.

ACKNOWLEDGMENTS

I am deeply indebted to Robert Rintz, managing director of Renard International USA (Los Angeles), a search firm specializing in the hospitality industry, for his interest. His important contributions to the book's concept and content are scattered throughout the chapters that follow, particularly the sections about new job searches, the résumé, networking, and other aspects of finding another job. His knowledge, enthusiasm, and energy brought much to these pages.

Thanks also to Edward E. Asawa, consultant to the Franklin D. Murphy Library of the Japanese American Cultural and Community Center in Los Angeles, for the historical information about Daruma dolls.

I am grateful to Dr. Gloria Spitalny and Dr. Stuart Clayman of the Power-sizing Consulting Group, in Boston, for the information about post-downsizing stress disorder (PDSD). Thanks also to my editors at Macmillan, Christina Buffamonte and Laura Uebelhor, for helping turn my manuscript into a real book. Special thanks to my irrepressible agent, Bert Holtje.

Finally, I want to thank Edythe, without whom not one word would have been written.

Martin Elkort
Los Angeles,
California
April, 1997

TABLE OF CONTENTS

INTRODUCTION

The very words are frightening: *Terminate*, to bring something (your job), or someone (you) to an end. *Severance*, the act of cutting something off (decapitation?). *Downsized*, "Honey, I shrunk the staff!" Or *fired*, to destroy by violent means (as in *firing squad*). But words can have other meanings, as can the situations they symbolize. Getting terminated may mean ending what was wrong to begin with; fired also means launched, as a missile or rocket ship, free to explore the unknown, or liveliness and vivacity of imagination (as in *fired with enthusiasm*), the ability to happily visualize what might now be possible. How you survive getting fired depends on you. It may be the worst thing that ever happened. But it could be the very twist of fate you needed, even though it doesn't seem so at the time.

If you have just been or are about to be fired, this book is for you. If your job is secure and you think there is no possibility of being fired, this book is for you. The message that runs through the book is simply this: Being fired is traumatic and unfortunate, but it has happened to millions of other good people besides yourself. There are tested ways not only to survive being fired, even as you seem to feel that your world is crumbling into ashes as you watch, but to prosper from the experience. To be able to treat your firing as a stumbling block on the road to success rather than the dead end of the pavement is not only possible, it is done by hundreds of people like you, every day. Here you will find proven techniques to overcome the firing, ways to organize your job search, and a plan for financial independence that will prevent your ever being fired again.

This book stresses the positive. When you are fired, positive is the only way you must think. To do otherwise would put the average person into an unhealthy emotional depression and dampen efforts to find the next job. But it would be unrealistic to totally eliminate the negative and observe the world of business with an uncritical eye, ignoring its dangers for the unwary employee. According to an article in *The Atlantic Monthly*,[1] we may soon enter a recession that could turn into an economic depression the likes of which have not been seen since the Great Depression of the thirties.

As wages continue to plummet, layoffs and firings continue apace, albeit at a slower rate, even with companies that don't really need to fire any employees to remain healthy. Companies, like individuals, play follow the leader and are fad-followers when it comes to certain practices like employee relations. Some companies fired so many people that they damaged the company and had to rehire again, to management's chagrin. The failed policies of both political parties, according to the article, led to a weakening or abandonment of fiscal restraints that kept recessions from getting out of hand for over fifty years. We have gone from a golden economy to a leaden economy. A recession that turns into a depression will mean that millions more will lose their jobs, and in an era when computerization, automation, outsourcing, and other changes have eliminated millions of jobs, the situation could become grimmer yet. Even if you hold on to your job, you will probably be in the job market sooner than you think. The number of workers who change jobs each year has grown 25 percent since 1990. Expect to switch jobs at least five times before you retire and expect to work on average eight years in each job. In 1990 the average length of stay on one job was eleven years.

There is a downward trend in unemployment that could wipe out the problem of unemployment—if life were as tidy as statistical trends make it seem. But continuing layoffs keep the ideal state of zero unemployment from ever being reached, as well as the usual reasons that operate in the real world to create job loss. According to the government Bureau of Labor Statistics, there are six basic types of unemployed people:

1. New Entrants. Bright-eyed and hopeful, they are entering the work force for the first time, many in low-level jobs with hopes of working themselves up to the top. Some will—most won't. 11.8%

2. Persons who completed temporary jobs. Hired for a short time, they are again out looking and hoping. 9%

3. On temporary layoff. They are hanging around the house, waiting for the expected call to return to work, and hoping. 11.8%

4. Re-entrants. This is by far the largest proportion of the unemployed. They all had jobs and were either laid off or had to stop working for some other reason. Some of them can no longer afford to keep going and have become part of the legion of the homeless. Because they are out of work they lost their car and/or mortgage. Many will never go back to work again, but most are hoping for a miracle. 36.8%

5. Job leavers. These are people who retired on a pension or Social Security, or who quit their jobs for other reasons and are no longer working. Most of them will never work again. 10.5%

6. Permanent job losers. This is the army of the fired, the downsized, the early forced retirement, victims of outsourcing. They want to get back in the work force but don't know how, can't find a job, and are slowly going downhill on the socioeconomic scale.

Most people think they will go through their working careers in a bubble of security. In reality, it's more akin to a tightrope balancing act. One misstep and down they go! It is a serious business, not to be taken lightly.

If you place something as valuable as the security of your job in the hands of employers who brag about being lean and mean managers, you shouldn't be surprised when they don't take good care of you. *You* are the only one you can count on for job security. You have already demonstrated intelligent concern by reading this book. When you are finished reading, make plans for the eventuality of getting fired, read all the other books on the subject you can find (they all have a different "take" and different ideas), and do everything you can to be, like a good scout, always prepared and always alert. You owe it to yourself and those you love.

Getting From Fired to Hired is a guide through the maelstrom of losing a job and offers a way to put the pieces of your working life back together after the living death of being fired. It takes you through the process:

- the warning signs
- the actual event
- the immediate aftermath
- how to handle it
- the long-range view of what to do with the rest of your career

This is not just another "how to" book. What is needed as you go through this experience is a way of holding on until the roller coaster comes safely to rest, a way of staying sane and whole while the furies rage, and a way to land on your feet, possibly in a better situation than the one you left. This may mean picking up the pieces and going back into the same career path, or it could signal a whole, new direction.

Getting from Fired to Hired is written with the sympathy and understanding of one who has been fired more than once and who also has had the uncomfortable experience of having had to fire people, the most unpleasant task facing employers and managers short of getting fired or going bankrupt. *Getting from Fired to Hired* is written by one who was at ground zero for the firing.*

My harrowing, climactic firing as executive vice-president of an association with international visibility took place two weeks before Christmas, when my children were on their way home for the holidays and I had just signed a two-year lease on an apartment, based on false assurances two months previously from my directors that my position

---

*People get fired for the oddest reasons. I was fired for the first time in the late 1950s from my job as disc jockey for a station in Santa Fe, New Mexico. I had played a Danny Kaye record called *Farming*, which satirized the way Hollywood actors were becoming dilettante farmers. Danny sang about a bull allegedly owned by George Raft. The actor's cows never calfed, according to the song, because Raft's bull was gay. This so offended the sensibilities of an important listener that I lost my job for the unintended offense.

was secure. At that time, as I found out later, my fate had already been decided. Never underestimate corporate duplicity. And never underestimate your own capacity for gullibility. I told them I was about to sign a two-year apartment lease and wanted to know if my job was secure. For them to tell the truth would have forced the issue. So they lied. No problem.

Later I wondered what it was that prompted me to ask the question. If my job was secure, why was I worried? As the emotions receded I realized that the clues were right there, in front of me. One director actually *told* me that I was going to be fired! What could be clearer than that? He was a great kidder, that one, a guy who would tell you something outrageous just to get your reaction. The life of the party. He had to be kidding, right? This time he wasn't. Like the townspeople in the fable "The Boy Who Cried Wolf," I didn't believe him this time. There are *always* clues that all is not well, if we would only see them. We shall look into these hints further on. They're crucial to job security.

As I write this, twenty-five years after the firing that changed my life, the feelings of anger, shame, and desperation that dominated my emotions in the weeks and months afterward come flowing back, unbidden, from some hidden recess of my mind with almost the same brutal force as when it actually happened. The men who did the deed are mostly dead or retired now, but I can still see them in my mind's eye and recall every detail in that small, overheated room, even their smells: body odor, old leather, and dust. Although the wounds healed long ago, the scars remain.

Your ears are burning and your knuckles are white as you walk down the street . . . away from the job you once were so eager to get and now will never return to. You need to reconnect with your life. But first, it's time to let off steam, time to get the hurt out of your system. Run until you're exhausted, go to the gym, get tanked with your friends, take in an action movie, down some fiery kung pao chicken or a spicy tuna hand roll or three, with lots of wasabe! Make love to your mate. Take a short vacation. Sure, you won't get paid this time, but didn't you earn it; don't you deserve it? Meet your kids, if you have any. They'll make you forget your troubles. Rediscover your kitchen—bake some bread. As you knead and pound the dough, pretend it's your former boss. You'll have time later to register for unemployment, go to the labor board or an attorney (if that's indicated), update your résumé, and scan the want ads.

What you must not do is *nothing*. Retreating inside yourself to nurse your wounds is fine . . . for five minutes. More than that runs the risk of sliding into self-pity and depression. Whatever you decide to do at this time—do it now. Keep the momentum going, even if you're only letting off steam. But if you don't want to go to a doctor or a psychologist, now is the time to reassert command of your mind and body. Life is good. Smell the roses.

When the psychoanalyst Carl Jung was told by a patient that he had just been fired from his job, he is said to have replied, "Congratulations!" When a patient told him that he had just been promoted in his job, Jung replied, "We must talk about this." Being fired from a job, especially for someone who has no idea that it is coming and who believes he or she is doing a good job and has been told so by his "superiors," is one of life's most devastating experiences, short of dying, that one can undergo. It has the destructive force of a bullet (perhaps that's why it's called *getting fired*), and goes to the heart of one's self-image, how one relates to relatives, friends, and colleagues. It can destroy marriages, dissolve friendships, and cause feelings of guilt and inadequacy that last a lifetime.

It has caused the death of more than one person at their own hands or as a result of stress-related illness. To cite just two examples, the guitarist and songwriter Doug Hopkins, of the group Gin Blossoms (he wrote their hit song, "Hey, Jealousy!"), became so difficult that he was fired. He committed suicide in 1993. When a major bank announced plans to fire 2,000 employees, two of them committed suicide.

Getting fired can be a tragedy. It's difficult to conceive of a person's taking his life because he was fired, valuing his job more than his life, more than his mate, more than his family and friends, and willing to saddle them with the psychological and material damage that the survivors must cope with for the rest of their lives. In *The Country Girl*, the playwright Clifford Odets has one of his characters, an alcoholic, say that anyone can make a decision, but it takes a true hero to live from day to day. Suicide requires nerve, not heroism, but it's really a selfish and cowardly way out of life's responsibilities.

Being fired is a major violation of the integrity of your personality. It (temporarily) violates and disrupts how you see yourself as a human being. It has been compared by psychologists to the loss of a loved one or the ending of a marriage, so there's not much point in compounding the crime by adding self-murder. It's natural for the thought of suicide to occur when you are in the depths of despair. ("They'll be sorry after I'm gone.") You're only human, after all. But if you find yourself lying awake at night considering which method is the quickest and most painless, you're in deep trouble. Get yourself to a doctor or psychologist immediately.

But being fired can also be an opportunity, as Jung wisely knew. It's a chance to break the mold, get out of the rat race, examine one's life, and perhaps set, or reset, career and lifetime goals. I went into severe depression after my experience, followed by analysis, medication, and many visits to lawyers, doctors, and anyone willing to listen to my tale of woe.

My healing began in the office of a lawyer, a fine, soft-spoken man with an ill-fitting gray toupee that covered a head full of wisdom. After hearing all the details and asking the appropriate questions, he rendered his opinion. "You have a good case," he told me. "There's an eighty to ninety percent chance of winning . . . very good odds. However, it will take a long time, perhaps eight to ten years, and they will defend themselves aggressively. You will be living, eating, and sleeping this case seven days a week during this time. You'll devote a big piece of your life to getting revenge. In the end, you'll probably win and collect a handsome settlement."

But it was what he said next that changed my life. "I'll take the case and sue them. But my advice is not to. You have the best part of your life ahead. Don't rehash the past. They did you dirty and they should pay, but are you the one to do it? Do you want to subject yourself, your wife, and children to this ordeal because your family will live through it, too? Look to your future happiness, not your past misery. Sure, it's an injustice, but you're still young and healthy and you'll do a lot better if you forget this, put it behind you, and get on with your life."

After a period of career floundering, we moved to a different state, bought a failing business, made a success of it, and sold it for a nice profit. I decided then to follow my first love and devote the rest of my life to writing. This is my second book. I have not looked back.

This book is for those who have just lost their jobs, or who are about to, as well as those trapped in the wrong job, fed up with their situation but not certain what to do next, perhaps afraid, like Hamlet, to chance the unknown. It's a book for those who, like the indomitable Daruma dolls of Japan, have the ability to "take a licking and keep on ticking," and the flexibility to learn from experience. Everyone has this innate ability, but many are unable to summon it up when needed. I have it and you have it, and you *will* survive this and perhaps a lot more in your life. Read on.

"It builds character," the coach Knute Rockne remarked after being asked why his team's losing streak did not make him unhappy. Getting fired can make you feel as if you have just been pushed off a cliff. But—properly handled—it can be a launching pad for the rest of your life, a chance to correct mistakes made earlier, an opportunity for fulfillment, the moment to take control of your life, to mature. In these trying times, companies justify their greed by announcing that they are downsizing, outsourcing, and becoming leaner and meaner, with the accent on the "meaner." Automation and computerization are changing the nature of the work force permanently in new and untested ways. Many traditional careers are going the way of the sail maker and blacksmith. Getting fired these days might be the best thing that ever happened to you.

DUE TO CONDITIONS BEYOND OUR CONTROL

2

The hapless swimmer caught in an undertow and swept out to sea is not thinking at the time that distant, impersonal forces beyond her or anyone else's control may be at fault, such as the gravitational pull of the moon or the invisible movement of underwater currents, or storm conditions caused by a hurricane five hundred miles away. What she needs—and needs now—is a lifeguard to rescue her. After the rescue, however, the infinite capacity we humans have of rationalizing and explaining the events in our lives takes over once again. As the steaming coffee soothes us we begin the search for answers to why it happened, the clues to unravel the eternal mystery of "why me?"

We cannot become unfired or erase the terrible pain we feel if we learn that it wasn't our fault, that we weren't fired because there is something wrong with us, a character flaw or lack of some sort. (Although sometimes it is, deep down, really our fault. If you suspect it to be operative in your case, get to work on it immediately, before it does more damage.) There is a demon in each of us that remains hidden in the dark recesses of our psyches. In times of stress it emerges to flash its pointed fangs. Many successful people secretly suspect that they are frauds, about to be unmasked, and wonder how they managed to fool everybody into thinking they were experts in the first place, even if they really were! This amazing paradox is mirrored in the emotions some feel when they get fired from a job. Someone has penetrated the curtain and unmasked us like Toto did to the Wizard of Oz, to discover that we are really a mass of weakness and indecision. That is why it is important to try to understand the impersonal forces behind some firings. Unless they were for emotional reasons or major transgressions on someone's part, they may be "due to conditions beyond our control."

If the reason for your firing is not readily apparent to you, or even to the person who fired you, it may well have been caused by complex economic conditions. Grasping the reality of this reason for losing your job will enable you to heave a huge sigh of relief. While it won't get you your old job back, it may lift a burden of guilt from your shoulders that you shouldn't have been carrying around in the first place.

Why have so many people been getting fired lately? Are there real reasons for it? Is it attributable to corporate greed or perhaps the impending end of the millennium—some mystical doomsday scenario that requires your being fired before it can be completed? As tempting as it may be to blame our job loss on flying saucers, the real explanation for much job loss today often lies in the arena of economics and social transformation. The good news is that the rate of firings has slowed down and perhaps permanently peaked, at least for what economists call the foreseeable future.

As we hurtle pell-mell into that future, we can't see where we are going, but we can rather quickly sort out events that impact us, with the assistance of professional explainers. One reason is that the Cold War is over, and with the end of the Communist threat hundreds of thousands of jobs were lost. While this may have had nothing to do with your non-Cold War–related job, it probably did have some impact because of the ripple effect. When a defense plant worker loses her job, she stops buying consumer and other items. Soon the people who make those items find themselves out of work, and so on down the line until it reaches you.

Like the story of how the cat got kicked, it had nothing to do with the cat, except as unwitting victim. Jobs once dependent on the Cold War and peripheral jobs dependent on *them* are, like the Cold War itself, history.

A second reason for much job attrition today is the impact of computers and automation on the work force. It doesn't take a rocket scientist, as our congressmen are fond of saying, to understand that if a computer can talk to you on the telephone and give you the phone number you request, someone just lost a job. If a robot is now bolting a motor into an automobile chassis down at the auto plant, someone just lost a job. Perhaps several people lost jobs, since one robot can work all three shifts without rest or overtime.

The third reason is the long-heralded arrival of the Information Age, made possible by the same computers and automation. The Industrial Revolution around a century and a half ago transformed our country from an agrarian, farming economy to an industrial one. Farm-related jobs were lost as blacksmiths, harness makers, and field hands migrated to the big city to get the exciting, new jobs available at the local factory. The smoking factory chimney replaced the plow as the symbol of America's greatness. (It's about to be replaced again, mainly for environmental reasons this time.) Labor-intensive jobs vanished as machines took over the back-breaking jobs of yesteryear.

We are living through similar, profound changes as the Industrial Age wanes and the Information Age emerges. The tiny computer chip wields the same power over our lives that the tractor and other revolutionary devices wielded in their day. Like it or not, a new age is upon us. Those who can't understand or refuse to accept it are doomed to be left behind, alone and muttering under their breath like the benighted Unabomber deploring progress in his filthy log cabin. Could the harness maker who stood at the side of the road and shouted "Get a horse!" at the occasional passing automobile as it clanked by possibly have guessed, only a hundred years ago, that the automobile he scorned would transform the entire country until it accounted for one-fifth of the economy? Did the fifth-generation sail maker perceive, as he stood on the pier watching the arrival of the first steamship over a century ago, that unless he abandoned his family business and learned how to be a steamfitter he would soon be out of work?

The office clerk with his green eyeshade and inkwells gave way to the stenographer with her shorthand pad and typewriter, who in turn gave way to the computer clerk and her mouse. The typographer, setting each sentence into a type slug, one letter at a time, gave way to the linotyper and the newspaper sketch artist lost his job unless he took up the new and revolutionary technology of photography.

Similar far-reaching changes are taking place today as the tectonic plates that support our economy shift yet again in earth-moving proportions. High school nerds with pocket protectors have become millionaires overnight because they invented a computer or a bit of software, words that didn't even exist until recent developments brought them forth. Ten years ago almost no one had heard of the Internet. Today politicians mention it casually in speeches and the odd network of interrelated computers has spread around the world and is responsible for hundreds of thousands of jobs. Nothing seems exempt from this inexorable technological march.

The medical profession, once dominated by the neighborhood physician and his little black bag, is now a vast, industrialized empire driven by sophisticated, computerized, state-of-the-art equipment, giant business-dominated health-care corporations, and huge drug companies, all spinning seemingly out of control by the daily discovery of new drugs, new treatments, new electronic devices . . . and even new diseases.

What hasn't changed is the impact on the work force. As we enter this exciting and sometimes scary world of tomorrow, millions of jobs have been lost and many thousands of people, unable to change for many reasons, some (such as age) beyond their control, may never hold a job again for the rest of their lives. But as old occupations and professions go into the trash bin of history, new ones emerge. These jobs will be mastered by those who can make the change and will become part of the establishment, to await the next turn of the corporate technological screw.

When the Industrial Revolution reared its head, a counter-revolutionary force emerged to fight it. Named after its founder, Ned Ludd, the Luddites went around smashing the new mechanical looms and other weaving machinery that threatened their jobs. Like Don Quixote tilting at windmills, they were no more successful in turning back the march of progress than the mad Unabomber, with similar goals, was today.

That jobs were lost—unfair and cruel as it was to the people who lost them—was inevitable. It is true that under the umbrella of the changes taking place and the see-no-evil attitude of many lawmakers, corporate greed is having a field day and companies are firing workers with an abandon not seen since early in this century. This has reinvigorated the moribund labor union movement and galvanized a new wave of worker discontent that may create a lot of unpleasantness before it runs its course.

So what? You are still unemployed and looking for work. It's cold comfort to realize that there may have been logical reasons for what happened to you. But any comfort, cold or not, is better than no comfort. You're not alone in your misery.

And you didn't bring it on yourself.

THE DARUMA PRINCIPLE

3

Our greatest glory is not in never falling, but in rising every time we fall.

—Confucius

An author can sometimes get a reader's attention by using the word *Zen* in a book title. What has walking the plank out the corporate window got to do with Zen Buddhism? Quite a bit, actually. Japanese business and political culture, for example, is saturated with what might be called the Daruma Doll Principle of Zen Buddhism—the admirable trait of being able to bounce back after adversity, time after time.

Japanese Daruma dolls are made of papier-mâché and come in all sizes from three inches high to the size of a small child. They are shaped like squat bowling pins or, if you recall the comic strip *L'il Abner*, like *schmoos*, those bulbous creatures whose job it was to make people happy, at whatever cost to themselves. Daruma dolls gaze blandly at the world like miniature Orphan Annies through huge, vacant eyes whose pupils are absent. When you buy a Daruma doll, you paint in one pupil with a marking pen or brush and put the doll in a prominent place in your home. In Japan it goes into the family shrine, a feature of most homes. Politicians paint in the first eye when they announce a run for office; businesspeople when they embark upon a new project. In the context of this book, you would paint in the first pupil when you start to look for your next career position. When you reach your goal, you paint in the other pupil and retire the Daruma, whose job is, happily, over. Then you buy a bigger Daruma for the next goal you set. To forestall an unhealthy rehashing of the past, Darumas are ceremonially burned at the end of each year.

The Daruma's presence is a constant reminder of your challenge and the task you face. He remains unfinished and partially sighted until you accomplish your goal and give him the gift of sight. He is a passive reminder and an inspiration. Every time you look at him, he returns your gaze with a baleful one-eyed reproach, inspiring you to redouble your efforts to reach your goal and give him the gift of full vision. As innocuous toys they have made generations of children happy.

They are also treasured by adults because they symbolize an admirable character trait. No matter how often you push them over, or how hard you push, they spring back to their original, upright positions. The secret is a weight hidden in each doll's rounded bottom. Their heavy base and low center of gravity keep them from falling over. They are unconquerable, enduring.

The Daruma doll is an example of Zen Buddhism in action. Painting in one eye and not the other sets up a tension and a boundary within which you can picture your goal and are free to move toward it. His one-eyed stare is a reminder of the task you committed yourself to and that you must complete. His ability to bounce back time after time is what you will go through as you get job rejection after job rejection. (Hopefully, not too many.)

The dynamic tension created by this harmless fluff of painted papier-mâché is very real and inspires continuation, staying with the plan when things look bleakest. When, like the Daruma, you bounce back for the last time and finally get the job you seek—and you will if you keep coming back—the satisfaction you will get from painting in the second pupil is wonderful to experience. You have given him vision, at the same time celebrating your own vision and spirit. You have proven to yourself, through the use of this funny little symbol of eternal hope, that you have staying power and the grit to hang in and keep going until you have reached your goal: a good job, maybe even a better job than the one you just left. You have traveled the sad road from the humiliation of being fired to the happy vindication of gainful employment. The distance between the Daruma's first eye and the second is only an inch or two, but what a long and difficult journey they bear witness to!

In the sixth century, an Indian monk called Bodhidharma, after nine years of contemplation in China, had a revelation out of which came the idea of Zen Buddhism. From China, Zen Buddhism migrated to Japan, where Bodhidharma is called Daruma. As the centuries passed, his story grew in the popular imagination and was embellished with charming, if sometimes gruesome details. For nine years, goes the legend, Daruma sat facing a blank wall in the monastery of Shaolin, unmoving, and so annoyed was he at the uncontrolled blinking of his eyes that he cut off his eyelids and cast them to the ground. Two tea plants sprouted where the eyelids landed, thus bringing tea to the world. Zen monks today sip tea to clear their minds and keep themselves awake during meditation. At the end of his nine-year meditation, Daruma found that his legs had shriveled up and fallen away. Subsequently, a monk called Hui K'o (or Eka) cut off his arm to demonstrate his determination to properly follow the way of the Daruma. Although Daruma long ago entered the mists of legend, he is believed by historians to have actually existed and to have died around A.D. 530.

Today, Daruma's legless legend is part of the cultural fabric of Japan. Daruma-dera, Zen temples that specialize in the production of the little dolls, are everywhere, and there is an annual Daruma festival in Gumma Prefecture that draws thousands of Daruma enthusiasts. When you enter into a business deal in Japan, you do so "with both eyes open," like the little Zen monk. "Seven times pushed over, eight times it rises" is the old Daruma proverb. Its roly-poly shape influenced the design of Japanese stoves and whiskey bottles and even entered the popular vernacular as a euphemism for prostitute, the Japanese equivalent of "round heels." When Japanese children play the universal children's game of staring at each other until one of them laughs, they often chant a two-line ditty in honor of Daruma, the quintessential starer. Watch closely the next time you see a Japanese politician celebrating victory in an election news report on television, and you may see the second eye being painted in.*

Daruma dolls are sold in stores specializing in Japanese items. If such a store is not available in your neighborhood, you may order one from: The Center Shop, Japanese American Cultural and Community Center, 244 South San Pedro Street, Los Angeles, CA 90012 (telephone 213/628-2725). The average price for a small doll is about $6, plus tax (and shipping, if required).

THE DARUMA PRINCIPLE IN ACTION

The Uses of Adversity

How we react to getting fired often depends upon how we look at life. A woman had twin seven-year-old sons, one an unquenchable optimist and the other a born pessimist. She took them to a child psychologist to find out why they were such opposites. The psychologist took the pessimist and put him in a stable behind his house. After an hour he went back to see how the boy was doing. He found the child in tears. "This happens all the time," wailed the boy. "Everywhere I go, something terrible happens. Now I have to stay in this smelly room full of horse doo!"

The psychologist took him back to the office and put the optimist in the stable. After an hour he went back to check on him. He found the second twin throwing horse manure around the stable with abandon. "Why are you so happy?" asked the psychologist. Gleefully, the child replied, "I figure, with all this horse manure, there's got to be a pony in here somewhere!" If you're like the first boy, getting fired is going to be exceedingly difficult to manage. But if you habitually look at the bright side of things, you'll do fine.

Steve Deutsch was fired from a good job in the clothing industry in New York. From his former employer's office he drove his beat-up old car straight to a dealer and traded it in for a brand-new vehicle, even though he knew he would not be able to make the payments beyond six months.

"If you drive to a job interview in an old, beat-up car, you go into the meeting in a beat-up and weaker position," he explained to me. "I needed to project self-confidence and nothing does it better for me than to pull up to a prospective employer's office in a shiny, new automobile. You get out of that car and you feel great, ready to take on the world. And if your prospective employer happens to see you drive up, he or she already has a positive opinion of you before you're even inside the building. Besides," he went on, "knowing that I am obligated to make car loan payments is a powerful reason to get another job quickly, and that reflects in my attitude during the interview. Employers can sense a loser before he opens his mouth," says this expert in sales.

"I got a job two weeks later, better than the one I had been fired from," he continued, "and I was stunned when my new employer told me that a company car came with the job. Now I had two cars: one that cost me nothing to own and operate and the other I would owe money on for the next three years.

"That night, as we celebrated in a nice restaurant, I told my wife that I thought it was time to get the swimming pool we wanted. A few days later, the guy came over to give us an estimate on the pool and admired my car in the driveway. I handed him the keys and told him to drive it around the block. When he got back, I asked him what he thought. He said that he would give anything to have a car like that. I said, 'Sit down!'

"When we had finished talking, I had traded him the equity I had in the car for a big chunk of what the pool would cost, and he took over the car loan. It's all in the way you see yourself," Deutsch said. "When life throws lemons at you, you learn to make lemonade real quick," he concluded, with a twinkle in his eye.

Real-Life Darumas

That unsinkable quality, the ability to survive a firing, is latent in us all. Here are some real-life Darumas who endured the ultimate rejection, survived their humiliating firings, and came back to greater triumphs. Some of them are world famous, and you have probably never heard of others. But they all share a similar trait—they are unsinkable. No matter what adversity they faced (usually getting fired or its equivalent) they bounced back, filled with plans and ready for action.

LEE IACOCCA   Fired as vice president of the Ford Motor Company by Henry Ford II, Iacocca, who created the company's now-classic Ford Mustang, roared back to corporate life as CEO of Chrysler Motors, wrote a million-dollar best-seller and led the campaign to save the Statue of Liberty. If you haven't read his book, *Iacocca*[1], and you've just been fired, get a copy and read it. It will make you feel better, and you may identify with many of the stories he tells, particularly how cruelly and brutally he was fired by Henry Ford and his brother, Bill. This chapter alone, a primer on how to handle yourself during your own firing, is worth the price of the book. In his tough, streetwise way he is touching and sometimes hilarious, as when he earthily describes the appearance of the two brothers as he walked in to be fired: "[They] were sitting at a marble conference table with an 'I smell shit' look on their faces." (page 126) Despite being responsible for the two best years in the company's history, he was fired on a whim. When he pressed Ford for reasons, the automobile mogul couldn't come up with any. Iacocca persisted until Ford lamely said, "Well, sometimes you just don't like somebody." (page 127)

STEVE JOBS   Fired as president of Apple Computer, the company he created around the famed Macintosh computer, which he also invented, Jobs is back as president of Pixar Corporation, whose first feature-length film, *Toy Story* (with Disney), was a box office smash. Jobs's stock in the new company is worth over $1 billion, far more than he ever earned at Apple Computer. It must have been a delicious irony for Jobs when Apple Computer recently asked him to come back and lend his talents to the company once again.

DALTON TRUMBO   One of the Hollywood Ten, Trumbo saw his career as a screen writer end when he was blacklisted (fired) after taking the Fifth Amendment and refusing to testify in hearings held by the House

Un-American Activities Committee in 1947. Trumbo bounced back under a pseudonym and wrote such films as *The Brave One* (1956), for which his pseudonym Robert Rich won an Oscar, *Roman Holiday, Spartacus,* and *Papillon.*

WINSTON CHURCHILL   Fired as first lord of the Admiralty after he was blamed for the disaster at Gallipoli in World War I and fired again from the Conservative Party in the thirties, he went on to become prime minister and lead his country to victory in World War II. He is considered today as one of England's greatest men.

NAPOLEON   Put in jail (fired) to get rid of him, he was later sent to Egypt (fired again) in the hope that he wouldn't come back. He did, as the most powerful figure in Europe, and became emperor.

CHARLES DREYFUS   A victim of anti-Semitism, Dreyfus was drummed out of the French army on trumped-up charges and publicly humiliated, then sent to Devil's Island prison. His "firing" so inflamed Emile Zola, a witness to the sorry spectacle, that he wrote his famous "J'Accuse" polemic. Another spectator, Theodore Herzl, was inspired to create the Zionist movement which, a century later, led to the formation of the state of Israel. Dreyfus was later pardoned and lived the rest of his life in peace.

MURRAY VIDOCKLER   The principal founder of British Caledonian Airlines (now owned by British Air) got the idea for the venture in Brooklyn, New York, where he owned a travel agency and a bus tour company. The airline caught on and grew rapidly, and Vidockler soon found himself the only American on the board of directors of a very large, now completely British company. How he was fired from the airline he started would take a whole book to tell, but fired he was. Vidockler went on to found the Society for the Advancement of Travel for the Handicapped, the Africa Travel Association, and a half dozen more organizations and magazines devoted to some aspect of the travel industry. In 1996 he was inducted into the prestigious Travel Hall of Fame, its highest honor, by the American Society of Travel Agents. He is planning greater things to come.

BILL SANDERS   Sanders was once riding high as director of information services for Candle Corporation, where he earned $140,000 a year plus the usual perks that go with such a job. He was responsible for the activities of 200 people in his division, but he lost his job in 1990 when his company downsized. He pursued one job lead after another for more than a year and was determined to get his career back. But after a long, dry period of futile job searches, he decided to get "a" career back, rather than his old career. The roller coaster ride was far from over, however. He invested $225,000 in a fast-food franchise in Culver City, California, planning to use the initial franchise to found a management company that would eventually run many more such restaurants. The restaurant failed to catch on, so he sold it and cast about for something else. He realized that he was good at picking winning stocks, having made substantial gains while managing his own portfolio in his previous career. Today, Sanders is a broker in a West Coast office of Oppenheimer & Co. and again bringing in earnings in six figures. He manages the investments of over 150 clients, with only one assistant. Many of his clients were former business associates and friends he made in his old career. Sanders says, "It took me many years, but I think I finally wound up as the right peg in the right hole."[2]

DOLORES BLANTON and WILLIAM FORTI   In 1990 their employer, General Dynamics, asked them to head up E-Metrics, a new company that would concentrate on new computer technology.[3] They were promised equity in the venture. But two years later, Hughes Aircraft bought the missile division of the company, along with E-Metrics, for $400 million. Bill Forti and Dolores Blanton were not compensated for their equity interest, and when the new owners closed the Pomona, California-based division, they were fired!* They sued, but the company denied making equity promises to the pair. The jury sided with the fired employees however, and in July 1996, awarded $3.7 million in compensatory damages and another $50 million each in punitive damages.

DON IMUS   Imus was fired as an obscure announcer working at an obscure radio station in Stockton, California, in the late 1960s for promoting an Eldridge Cleaver look-alike contest. A former homeless person who got his meals by checking for loose coins in telephones and vending machines, Imus overcame alcohol and drug abuse and now rivals Howard Stern as a nationally syndicated in-your-face talk show host. The radio shlock-jock's most recent notoriety came when he insulted President Clinton and the First Lady at a dinner in 1996. He is reportedly worth millions.

---

*Along with 125,000 other Southern California aerospace workers in an industry-wide shake-out.

RICHARD NIXON   Having endured the humiliation of losing his job as President of the United States and leaving office under a cloud, he rehabilitated himself and in the years before his death wrote several well-received books and advised presidents and politicians on foreign policy and other matters.

JEFFREY S. WIGAND   Fired from his $300,000-a-year job as Brown & Williamson Tobacco Corp.'s director of research and development, Wigand was the first senior executive in the tobacco industry to object publicly to the practices of his industry. Today he teaches Japanese and science at a high school in Louisville, Kentucky and was recently given the coveted Ethical Humanist Award by the Ethical Culture Society. His new salary is $30,000 a year. Wigand says that he has found "unexpected happiness and joy in adversity."[4]

JEFFREY KATZENBACH   Katzenbach may have gotten an ironic chuckle from Will Rogers's statement "All I know is what I read in the papers!" Katzenbach learned of his firing as chairman of Disney Studios from a press release handed out to the media. He consoled himself soon thereafter by becoming the middle-initial partner in SKG Dreamworks, a huge, new Hollywood studio which promises to be the biggest in the industry when completed. Other Disney executives who read about their firings in the morning trade papers include former TV chief Dennis Hightower and Hollywood Pictures head executive Michael Lynton.

GREEDSPEAK

In Hollywood, a safe rule of thumb is if someone claims in print that they love their work and are staying put, you can bet it's a code for "I'm outta here."

—Claudia Eller, *Los Angeles Times,* July 16, 1996

Greedspeak is related to doubletalk. But whereas doubletalk is meant to be funny, the sinister purpose of greedspeak is to confuse and mislead. It is most rampant in the military where, in a classic example, a U.S. Army officer in Vietnam explained that in order to save a village they had to destroy it. During Operation Desert Storm, American soldiers, making a tragic error, fired on and killed other American soldiers, mistaking them for the enemy. The episode was the result of friendly fire, said the military spokesman. There is nothing friendly about a bullet that kills you. Ethnic cleansing is another horrific euphemism, used to sanitize genocide and other crimes against humanity and to make them seem, somehow . . . nice.

Even more disconcerting than military greedspeak is the corporate rhetorical perversion of belief systems so that they justify or conceal the actions of executives as they rid their companies of unwanted employees while at the same time putting a verbal spin on the executive executions so that they seem harmless. Politicians love analogies to sports such as "leveling the playing field," "team players," and comparisons of legislative agendas to winning or losing a game. But corporate barons get right to the point, or in their case, the bottom line. Consider the remark made by Scott Paper CEO Albert J. Dunlap after one-third of the entire work force of his company, 10,500 jobs, had been, shall we say, wiped out. Dunlap explained, "It's a sin to lose money, a mortal sin."[1] Bad news for the board of directors and the accounting department, who may now have to spend eternity repenting in Hell for their failure to make money for Scott Paper Corporation.

Manipulation of language to mask the truth reaches epidemic proportions in American culture, but nowhere is it more common or threatening to the individual than in business. While everyone who hears it understands the real intent of the phrase, it somehow loses its sting by being cloaked in an innocuous euphemism. We are not speaking here about corporate slang. Every profession has its peculiar argot, the shortcut "in" words that encode and obfuscate common phrases in ways that indicate that the speaker is part of the corporate or professional culture, an insider. Slang words that mean fired, such as booted, sacked, canned, or axed are simply that: slang applied to job severance—gallows humor, corporate style. As such it is harmless, albeit tasteless. Greedspeak, which is simply an attempt to be hip, is more sinister than slang. Greedspeak is a deliberate perversion of language to further the aims of management or to hide its true meaning. Be alert to greedspeak. When you suspect that it's being used on you, try to decode it. Your job may be affected. Here are a few examples of standard corporatese used by management that you should be aware of:

- *Downsizing:* "We are firing 50% of our staff and making the rest work twice as hard to make up the difference."

- *Re-engineered:* "Our strategic planning engineers have come up with a plan to re-engineer and restructure the company, profitwise. Sorry to say, you'll have to go as part of the re-engineering. It's set in concrete now."

- *No-Fault Termination:* "Don't ask us for the reason we had to fire you, because we don't know either!"

- *Dynamic and synergistic:* "Our company is run by a clique of thirty-something yuppies who have had everyone over forty-five years old fired."

- *A Hard-Driving Environment:* "If you don't show up for work on Sunday, don't bother coming in on Monday."

- *Outsourcing:* "We are firing 400 assemblers who make $20 an hour and from now on will buy already assembled widgets from a company in Asia where employees are paid $40 a month for the same work."

- *Let Go:* As in "We had to let George go last week." The only reason old George managed to hang on this long was because management insisted on holding on to him. Management didn't want George to go, but they had to "let go" of him and watch him drift away . . . because he insisted.

- *Cashiered:* An archaic way of saying "fired." Instead of sending the hapless employee out into the storm, he was merely sent to the cashier to get his paycheck (his last one).

- *Laid off:* The implication is that you may be "laid on" again in the future. Then again, you may not. They're weasel words meaning fired.*

---

*The layoff originated during the Great Depression of the 1930s, according to Alan Downs, a management consultant (in his Corporate Executions [New York: Amacom, 1995], p.19). At that time, corporations temporarily suspended thousands of people from their jobs (many with a small stipend to help them through), with the intention of rehiring them when conditions improved. Being laid off during the Depression was not the same as being fired, which is permanent. Management's current use of the term laid off to denote what is actually a permanent firing thus becomes more acceptable to the public, which views the phrase as less harmful than firing. It's another perversion of language, aided by past acceptance of a term no longer relevant. Mass "layoffs" decimate the tax base of communities, hampering their ability to support and attract local industry with well-maintained streets, sewers, and schools. Consider what happened to Detroit when much of the automobile industry folded in the wake of surging Japanese imports. Or Eastman Kodak Company, which has restructured itself five times since 1985 at a total cost of over $2.1 billion and 12,000 jobs. Since then its profit margins have been halved, its stock price is not attractive, and its total revenues are not much larger than before restructuring.

- *Realignment:* "Somehow, our company got a little out of line, a bit unfocussed. After exhaustive study we found the reason to be you! If you would only move out of the way, we could realign the company again." It's another weasel word used when management cloaks the decision to fire you in euphemisms.

- *Bureaucracy:* The process of turning energy into solid waste.

- *Golden Parachute:* "We had to push him out of the plane, but we made it worth his while. We made him a consultant."

- *Golden Handshake:* "We parted as friends, but we slipped him a little something when we said good-bye."

- *Pension Fund:* Emergency money for corporate adventures.

- *Corporate Culture:* Do unto others before they do unto you.

- *Aggressive Go-Getter:* Someone not afraid to trample others to get to his or her goal.

- *Self-Starter:* An employee who does something without being told. (Just try it sometime.)

- *Ombudsman:* Someone everyone talks to but nobody listens to.

- *"Focus on our core competencies":* Translation: "We couldn't run this thing."[2]

- *"Unlock value for investors":* Translation: "We made stupid acquisitions, and now we're dumping them."[3]

- *"I take full responsibility!":* When a CEO makes this statement, it's résumé update time.

It's a Downsized World, After All!

When former California governor Jerry Brown told his constituents that they would have to lower their expectations, he was derided as "Governor Moonbeam." Similar derision met former President Jimmy Carter when he echoed comparable sentiments. In hindsight, they were on to something. The present epidemic of firings, downsizings, and outsourcings—a euphemism for buying from outside suppliers, often in other countries, to avoid having to hire people—put millions of workers in the ranks of the unemployed. This relieved management of its responsibility to the government for payroll taxes and its responsibility to its employees for health plans, retirement programs, and other financial obligations a company assumes when it hires people—not the least of which are salaries.

While companies prosper in the short run from downsizing and outsourcing, the phenomenon has ushered in many consequences: the rise of the two-career family, more latchkey kids more families losing their homes and crossing the poverty line, more homeless people on the streets, and more people getting fired all the time. That this is a negative way to attack problems becomes evident when it is realized that the millions of people who are now out of work were potential customers for everything made in America. They now can no longer afford to buy or even repair their cars and will not buy houses, with all the secondary purchases such as drapes and rugs, garden supplies, etc. Throwing millions of people out of work lowers the gross domestic product because it shrinks the market for consumer goods and services, thereby shrinking market share revenue of some of the very companies doing the firing.

Three million jobs have been eliminated since 1990, according to a 1996 estimate.[1] If the five million workers who became so discouraged they simply quit looking for work and the four and a half million who involuntarily must work part time are factored into what the government claimed at the start of 1996 was an unemployment rate of 5.6 percent, the real rate of unemployment rockets up to 14 percent—by definition a crisis.

To survive in today's business environment one must face certain realities. It will probably be some time before the economy gets past the spasms of change afflicting it and becomes more stable and salaries return to former levels; perhaps not in our professional lifetimes, perhaps never. It's also a fact of life, pundits tell us, that job security is a thing of the past. No longer will most people have a job for life from which they will eventually retire. From now on, "job security" refers only to the guard in the lobby of the building. In today's (and tomorrow's) world it is normal for people to change jobs every few years, we're told. That this leads inevitably to a lessening of company loyalty and a consequent loss of production and efficiency seems, unfortunately, not to be as important to today's management as immediate gains in the balance sheet, the much touted "bottom line."

Why Companies Are Shooting Themselves in the Foot

While the advantages to downsized companies are obvious, many don't seem to think the disadvantages are serious, or will be serious tomorrow.

Here are a few of the disadvantages corporations should consider when downsizing:

1. Loyalty to the company is replaced by loyalty to oneself as employees realize there is nobody in their corner but themselves.

2. Bad morale in the workplace leads to lower productivity and carelessness.

3. Labor shortages are created by downsizing highly skilled employees, whose training and skills took years to develop.

4. Overburdened management becomes so busy coping with day-to-day problems that they have no time for crucial long-term planning or strategic work.

5. Overworked support staffs.

6. Lack of job satisfaction, leading to unhappy employees constantly looking for a better job.

7. Not enough employees to properly service customers, resulting in unhappy customers, complaints, inefficiencies, wasted time, and inferior products.

8. The resurgence of formerly dormant labor unions, leading to conflict.

In a recent report, *NBC Nightly News* revealed that 49 percent of companies that had laid off significant numbers of employees experienced no increase in profits, 66 percent had no increase in productivity, and 86 percent suffered a decline in employee morale.

As the new millennium approaches the two letters—*A* and *D*—that accompany the date stand for something else in addition to Anno Domini. Welcome to the Age of Downsizing. You should install a smoke detector in your career, an emergency plan against the day you may be fired or quit. Install it the day after you're hired, and keep it in working order because you'll never know when disaster will strike. If this sounds cynical, it isn't. It's realistic. A company has well-thought-out plans and procedures for firing employees as part of its policy, and these bear the stamp of approval of the company's attorneys. You should do no less than have equally well-thought-out plans against the eventuality of your being fired. It's good business and good professional behavior that could save you a lot of grief (and money) when the expected unexpectedly happens. Just add it to the normal precautions you usually take, like buying life insurance and all those other things that are necessary, if unpleasant to think about.

At the same time, management should not be prejudged and should be presumed innocent until proven otherwise. To do less would condemn yourself to job paranoia and mind-poisoning unhappiness. Your responsibility is to the company that hired you. It pays your salary and deserves your loyalty and respect. But be a good scout: Be alert! As you go about your business at the office, be cheerful and cooperative but keep a weather eye out for storm warnings. Like any storm, the first signs are subtle, unexceptional, almost unnoticeable. But they will be there. Ignore them at your peril.

The Anxious Generation

Robert Reich, former U.S. secretary of labor, calls the new work force the "anxious generation": anxious about job security, anxious about their chances of getting ahead, anxious about vanishing benefits, anxious about their futures—and just plain anxious. His advice to career-builders? "Think of your career less as a ladder and more like a web."[2] He's not referring to the Internet. The traditional corporate ladder, that you work your way up, secure in your job, still exists, but it is in transition to the brave, new society we are told to prepare for. In the future, Reich suggests, those who get ahead will not be ladder-climbers but web-spinners. His intriguing metaphor likens today's working environment to a web, which has a center and many paths (skills, opportunities, career options) radiating from it. They (webs) are flexible, with changes taking place all the time.

Those who succeed in this environment will be nimble and acquire the many new skills that modern technology requires. The web allows its denizens to reach out, learn, develop contacts and friends in new areas, adapt to new ideas, and move not only from job to job but also from skill to skill. The traditional corporate ladder confines the worker to one rung at a time, one slot in the company that leads, inevitably, to promotion after promotion until retirement. When a ladder-percher is fired, he falls far and quickly, unless he has the prowess to swing rapidly onto another ladder. Web dwellers can move more flexibly and faster, not only into another job, but perhaps into a different career.*

Many companies today, to their credit, stubbornly conform to old-fashioned paternal authoritarianism. You come in at the bottom, work your way up, and retire with a top position: vice president, maybe even president. The pension fund is sacred, reserved for you and your colleagues. It's the company's responsibility to look after you as long as you do your job.

While the exceptions usually prove the rule, there is hope that management will eventually perceive that being kind to employees is good for business. In the summer of 1996 many companies that had downsized began to rehire. Some magazine articles made it seem as though management goofed by firing all those people and now, with egg on their corporate faces, they were rehiring to correct the imbalance in the work force.[3]

Corporate Anorexia

For every action there is an equal and opposite reaction, goes the law of physics, and it's beginning to evidence itself in the downsizing fever as well. The dehumanizing and destructive effects of this practice on society are drawing the wrath of both sides of the political spectrum. The *New York Times* recently ran a seven-part series on the subject, and magazines like *Newsweek* and *The Atlantic Monthly* have also taken aim at it.[4] The Republican presidential candidate Pat Buchanan has attacked "corporate butchers," disposable workers, and the downsizing of the American dream. The Democratic Secretary of Labor Robert Reich recommended the government give tax breaks to companies that treat employees decently. His suggestion has been taken up by Democrats in Congress, who introduced legislation for that purpose. The issue has been joined by the newly invigorated labor unions, and we should be hearing more about it from these sources and others in future.

There is an apocryphal story about a farmer trying to find the exact amount of feed for his prize bull so he could save money on the large feed bill. Each day he fed the bull one less teaspoonful of feed. "Things

It's worth noting that 95 percent of U.S. employees work in small businesses with fewer than one hundred employees, according to Robin Ryan, a career counselor in Seattle who is the author of 60 Seconds and You're Hired (Impact, $9.95). She advises career-builders to "Learn all the skills available, to be responsive to all the options out there, to watch for opportunities and jump into them" (quoted in the Chicago Tribune, August 4, 1996).

was agoin' great," he explained to a neighbor a few months later, "but the durned bull up and died right in the middle of the experiment!" Corporate anorexia has already hit many companies that let so many employees go that their productivity and competitiveness were affected. As the downturn in the economy slowly bottoms out, many companies are replacing employees that they let go in the firing frenzy of the early 1990s, usually with less qualified—but cheaper—workers.

In an effort to counter the bad press, some companies are trying to substitute more humane and sensible policies—retraining, incentives, shifting employees to other positions within the company, and stock options to give workers a stake in the company—for the brutal policies of decimating jobs through mass, impersonal firings. These are, unfortunately, the exceptions rather than the rule. What is more widespread is indiscriminate rehiring in an effort to correct what is regarded as a policy that may have placed the company in a less competitive position. It was following such corporate fads that led to the mass firings in the first place. Mindless rehiring can lead to overhiring, followed inevitably by another wave of firings, *ad infinitum.*

The Rewards of Corporate Virtue

The old values are still around in countless and unexpected places. When a textile plant in New England burned down recently, the owner, a principled septuagenarian who read from the Bible, the Talmud, and the works of William Shakespeare every night before retiring, could have fired his workers and retired on the insurance. Instead, he vowed to keep the plant open and the employees on salary, even though there was no place for them to work. He not only assured them continued paychecks, but gave each employee a hardship bonus. Result? The employees had the plant up and running in temporary quarters within a few weeks, and employee loyalty soared.

In 1987, John Tu, an immigrant from Shanghai, China, and David Sun, from Taiwan, founded Kingston Technology Corp., a computer memory board maker in Fountain Valley, California. Today it is the largest memory board maker in the world and has 60 percent of the U.S. market, among other things. The company prospered by combining technological prowess and aggressive sales efforts with a corporate culture based on putting employee needs before those of vendors. A plaque in the lobby urges employees to aspire to compassion, courtesy, modesty, and honesty. Among the benefits Sun and Tu provide are free lunches every Friday, golf outings, wages substantially higher than industry averages, plus many fringe benefits, generous bonuses, profit sharing, and a liberalized dress code that prohibits shorts but allows almost anything else within reason. They make major contributions to local organizations, handing out $400,000 checks in 1995 to the local school district and the Boys and Girls Club of Fountain Valley. They also set up a scholarship fund for low-income families.

They recently sold a controlling interest in Kingston to Softbank Corp. of Japan, which seems to have similar ideas. Sun and Tu celebrated the takeover by handing out $1,000 bonuses to all full-time employees and throwing a huge pizza party that night. They are mulling over plans that will allow their five hundred employees to share in the new takeover. Among the ideas being considered are employee trust funds, college funds, mortgage payoffs for workers, or bonuses equivalent to two years' salary. Their corporate philosophy is credited with bringing them from a startup investment of $4,000 in 1987 to a $1.5-billion powerhouse today. Their next sales goal is $2 billion, and with their unique corporate mixture of advanced technology, aggressive sales, and fanatic employee dedication, can anyone doubt they'll reach it?

TWENTY-ONE CLUES THAT YOU MAY BE FIRED

I had a good job, but I left!
I had a good job but I left!
First they hired me,
Then they fired me,
Then, by golly . . . I left!

—U.S. Army marching chant

You can be happily employed in your next job or, like the anonymous soldier in the marching chant, you can leave and join the army long before a decision is made to fire you. But to enjoy this important advantage over your employer you need to be a bit like Sherlock Holmes while you work. The imperturbable private eye was always on the lookout for something amiss, no matter what he was doing at the time, and immediately brought it to the attention of his perpetually baffled friend, Doctor Watson.

Give your job 100 percent of your attention, of course, but be alert to subtle changes in your environment, changes that may portend trouble. To prepare you for the job of sniffing out danger to your career, here are 21 clues to watch for. You won't need a magnifying glass to find them— just keep your eyes open and be alert. Any one of them may indicate a change in direction of management's plans for you. If you notice 2 or 3 of the clues present, begin your search for your next job immediately.

1. Your expected raise is delayed or canceled for flimsy reasons, if any reasons at all are offered. When it comes, it's not as large as you were led to believe it would be. Or your raise is not comparable with the raises of others in your company, many of whom may have been hired long after you were.

2. When a tough assignment comes up, you are not the one they want to tackle it. You're overlooked in favor of someone else.

3. Your job status, title, or responsibilities have been changed. Is it a step up the career ladder, a step sideways, or step backward?

4. You recently got on the bad side of your boss or supervisor.

5. The behavior of management seems to indicate that something important, or peculiar, is going on. There are a lot of closed-door meetings, whereas heretofore there have been very few meetings, and those were with the doors open. The comings and goings of management have an ominous feel to them. When you ask, innocently, "What's happening?" and the response is "Nothing," it's a danger signal. It may not involve you . . . yet. Perhaps the company is in the process of being purchased or is getting ready to file for bankruptcy. Or management may have made the decision that your entire department is going to be computerized, and everyone will be fired. In the meantime they need the department to continue functioning until they have everything in place. No way will management let this news out until they are ready to take action.

6. New employees have been assigned to your department, or to you personally, with instructions to teach them everything you know. Recently, some software companies imported workers from India and Pakistan as trainees. When the trainees had learned everything they needed to know, they were sent back to work for a

subsidiary company set up in their native country for the purpose. There they write software for one-tenth of the pay of American workers, communicating in real time with the American-based company with almost the same ease as if they were in the next room. Once they were in place, the American workers who trained them were fired.

7. Management has suddenly disappeared. You're left alone for long periods, whereas up to this time you saw your boss or supervisors on a daily or hourly basis.

8. Management has become mute. Interoffice memos have dried up, and usually gabby supervisors have stopped talking. To everyone, or just to you? In some companies, silence is a management tool: What you don't know won't hurt them. But if silence is not the rule in your company and suddenly you become aware that all has become quiet, be suspicious. A story went the rounds a few years ago of three company presidents who met at their club to discuss management theories. The first president said that he uses the pyramid system of management. He sits at the top of the pyramid and gives orders to his vice presidents, who pass them down to department heads, and so on down the line until they reach the workers arrayed at the bottom of the pyramid. The second president said that he uses the wheel theory of management. He is in the center of an imaginary wheel from which radiate spokes. Each spoke is a vice president, and the information goes out to the rim, where the workers are going around in circles. The third president chimed in that he uses the mushroom theory of management. "I keep 'em in the dark and every once in a while I throw some manure on 'em!"

9. Other employees have cut short their socializing with you. You catch them looking at you oddly (perhaps with sympathy?). Colleagues who routinely used to stop by your workstation to chat now walk silently past with eyes averted.

10. When you're in a meeting with your supervisor or boss, she takes notes, whereas heretofore she never did. The meetings often take place with a third party present. This ominous tipoff means that they want a corroborative witness to what you say. She may be constructing the company's defense about your behavior that

may be used against you as cause for firing you, or to defend themselves after you are fired in the event you bring suit. While the note-taking may be harmless, it's a danger signal if there were no such actions previously. Don't expect the notes to be in your favor, or even accurate. They represent management's case against you.

An employee of a small firm was recently asked to go into her boss's office in his absence to retrieve a certain document from his desk. In looking for it, she noticed a folder with her name on it. Curious, she opened the folder to see what was in it. What she saw sent her to a job counselor. In the folder was page after page of notes written during and after meetings with her, each meticulously dated and time stamped. The contents of the notes twisted her words and put words into her mouth that she never said. She quit shortly thereafter and was soon hired by another company at a higher salary.

11. Your boss has become irritable and curt whereas until now he or she was the soul of good cheer and friendliness. It could be mid-life crisis, but can you ignore it with confidence? Is your boss in trouble? Has she made some major mistakes recently? Even if your boss owns the company, her job may not be secure if she answers to a board of directors.

12. You have received written or verbal warnings about details of your work.

13. Your company's quarterly report shows poor earnings or otherwise indicates trouble for the firm.

14. Is your industry healthy? Are the newspapers and magazines full of stories about the problems in your industry? Reading business newspapers and magazines occasionally, such as the *Wall Street Journal, Barrons, Forbes, Fortune,* and many others, will keep you tuned in to developments in your field. Troubles in your industry may translate shortly into job insecurity for you. If your industry is in trouble and if your company in particular is mentioned, ratchet up the level of your research and read everything you can find about it. Go to the library and a good newsstand or bookstore. Find out who in your company handles the biggest accounts, and try to get to know them. You may discover, in casual

conversation, news that will lead to layoffs and your own eventual firing.

15. Your company is going through a wave of cost-cutting actions such as hiring freezes, elimination or reduction of travel benefits and employee training, across-the-board pay cuts, a rise in early retirements of senior employees, a "rethinking" of the company vacation policy that results in less vacation time, a new health plan that's cheaper than the old one but offers fewer benefits, a cut in allowable overtime hours, a flood of memos and e-mail urging the saving and recycling of office supplies, and the elimination of such perks as free coffee and other amenities. While none of these of itself may signal anything other than a healthy desire to rein in what management now considers excessive expenditures, the moves might be part of a pattern that may lead to a decision to cut staff expenses by firing people.

16. Your company has recently changed the way it does business, for example, by putting in computers. If it has, and you don't yet know how to work a computer, buy one now. Nobody gets fired faster than employees who cannot adapt to change, and computers are where it's at for the foreseeable future. Even if this has not yet happened, get involved with computers anyhow. When the time comes for them to enter your company, you'll be among the first to raise their hands (and maybe their salaries). Besides, you can get wonderful, inexpensive programs for them that type out professional-looking résumés. The Internet offers opportunities for job searching, among many other employment resources. You might find a job from the comfort of your home.

17. You are putting in longer and longer hours and still can't keep up with your work. You are always behind on delivery dates and deadlines.

18. You have recently developed physical ailments that could reasonably be attributed to tension, such as high blood pressure, stomach pains, unexplained headaches, sleeplessness, irritability. Can you logically attribute the tension to be job related? Perhaps your body is reacting to job-induced pressure and warning you through symptoms of something your conscious mind is denying. See your doctor before you come to any conclusions, but be alert to the possibilities.

19. A new senior manager has been hired for the company or for your department. The new broom syndrome may be about to afflict your department. The new manager will want to strengthen his position by bringing in people he knows and firing those whom he deems unknowns (enemies or at best, obstacles).

20. You are no longer as enthusiastic about your job as you were the day you were hired. You have become a clock-watcher. You can't wait to go home at night. You're starting to hate your job. Even if you don't think you'll be fired, it may be time to move on. Eight years with one company is a good level to make such a decision. If you are burned out or in the process of getting there, you can be sure that it will be noticed.

21. You're starting to feel like an outsider. No one cares about your opinions any more. You are being ignored for choice assignments while others are being chosen.

If you have become convinced that the firing bullet will soon have your name on it, you have some control over the situation at this time. You may not be able to stop the bullet, but you don't have to be there when it arrives. You still have the option of quitting your job once you know you'll soon be fired. The problem is, you don't have another job to go to and there may not be enough time to find one before you lose the one you now have. What to do? In most cases it's probably better to start a vigorous job hunt immediately and wait it out. There is always an outside chance you won't be fired, but then, as the list above indicates, you probably will be. If you leave voluntarily, the company doesn't have to give you any severance benefits, and you may not qualify for unemployment insurance. These are serious matters and may outweigh the risk of a humiliating firing and how to explain it on your résumé and in interviews for new jobs.

Disabuse yourself of any false ideas you may harbor about company loyalty. Management will soon show you how loyal they are to you, so don't mislead yourself about any obligation you think you have to them. You have only one obligation now: to yourself and your family. Do your job, keep your head down, and bend every effort toward getting another job. Time is on your side for the moment, but the sands are getting low and will run out soon. It would be a good idea at this time to prepare yourself for being fired by acting out your firing, with a friend you can trust playing the role of your employer. By such play-acting, you can rehearse several scenarios and get used to being fired, if only in make-believe, so when it comes, you'll at least be familiar with the drill and won't go into a state of shock. You can also work on your severance negotiations in this manner. This assumes, of course, that you have some advance suspicion that you're about to be discharged. Unfortunately, to many people it comes like a bolt from the blue.

STAYING COOL IN FRONT OF THE FIRING SQUAD

8

You have been cast adrift and are rudderless—for the moment. The lightning bolt that hit you numbed your mind, but now is no time for a nervous breakdown. Most people are optimists, always hoping for the best. That's why when you are fired it can hit you with traumatic force, derailing every logical premise you use to guide your life and career, wrenching your emotions and sometimes making you lose temporary control of them. An emotionally healthy person has a positive opinion of herself. She sees herself as special: an intelligent, talented person, an asset to any company. Egos sometimes get out of hand of course, but you must love yourself before others can love you, say the psychologists. A positive self-image is the sign of a healthy mind. When you are fired, the implication is that you have been weighed in the scales and found wanting, that you're not good enough to work here, you aren't liked any more.

This is a terrible implied judgment if it comes from one you dislike or fear, still worse if it comes from someone you like and thought liked you. Even if it's not your fault, and the firing is an impartial action of the company dictated by economic imperatives that have little or nothing to do with you, such as the loss of a major account or contract, it's difficult not to take this as an assault on your self-image. It's an evaluation of you as a human being that came up negative and recommends severance.

Why me, you think? You have been stripped of your dignity, your world is out of focus, your security torn asunder. How will you ever put the pieces together again, you wonder? Though you are temporarily adrift emotionally, this is the time to quickly get back in control. You can beat your breast and cry later. What you do in the few minutes following the breaking of the news of your firing is important. If you feel that you're losing it, leave the room. You don't need to explain or even say anything. Just leave! Go into the rest room until you regain your composure. Better still, go into the office of a fellow employee who is your friend, someone you trust. Close the door and sit down. Tell her to put her calls on hold. Now, go ahead and cry, curse, let off steam in a nondestructive way. Your friend will understand and offer comfort. If it's still too much for you to manage, go home for the day.* Everyone will understand. There will be time tomorrow to clean out your desk, to go to the person who fired you and apologize for your emotions. It may even put you in a better position to bargain for your severance package if they feel that you are emotionally distraught.

What you should *not* do is lose your temper. It's tempting to finally tell the boss what you think of him, that miserable, lying so-and-so! But by displaying anger you risk being branded an emotionally unstable hothead, an unreliable person. You hand management proof that firing you was a smart idea, and you weaken your negotiating position. Do *not* argue your case with the person firing you, either. Don't plead or beg for your job back or even try to defend yourself from whatever reason they give for firing you.† Above all, never threaten, or even clench your fists.

---

*If you drive home, make certain that you're calm enough to use the car. Don't take your frustrations out on the accelerator pedal.

---

†They will give you a reason, in most cases. If by some chance they don't, you should ask why the decision was made. Was it something you did? It's important for many reasons that they make this statement of why you were fired to you at the time you are discharged.

Any statement or act of belligerence weakens your position and may create serious problems. If you decide later to fight back, you may be tipping your hand by presenting your reasons now and giving them a chance to strengthen their position. Silence and a stiff upper lip are your best weapons for the moment. You have only two tasks now: to accept your firing and to bargain for the best deal you can get—everything you're entitled to and a bit more.

Stay with your optimism, but salt it with a touch of pessimism. Resist the temptation to let loose. You need all your wits about you to get through this period, and you don't want to do or say anything that will haunt you later or give your employer the upper hand. He already got the upper hand by firing you. But by maintaining your dignity and composure, you compel him to respect you, and you begin the process of taking the initiative. This is a precondition to coming into your severance negotiations from a position of strength, preposterous as it may seem at the moment.

The boss is not always right, but he is always the boss. Firing you is the ultimate proof of his power. You have few options—the situation is not under your control. But in this not-so-subtle exercise of power you can make him respect you by acting with dignity, decorum, and self-possession. This begins to tip the balance of power in your favor. If he at least respects you, he will be willing to listen to your demands and the reasons you give for them and may be disposed to be generous, or at least fair. A display of anger on your part may frighten him, or at the very least put him into a guarded position from which concessions in your favor become more difficult to obtain. By not allowing yourself the indulgence of anger, satisfying as it might momentarily be, you are actually, believe it or not, doing your ex-employer a favor by making his task less onerous. He is, despite what you may have heard around the water cooler, a human being with feelings. By taking the news like a mature person, you lift a burden, small though it may be, from your boss's shoulders. Now he owes you something. And you are about to demand it.

> If they don't, press them politely for the reason. Don't leave the meeting until you have their explanation of why you were discharged. If your discharge was for reasons beyond their control, such as the closure of your department, they should have no objection to telling you. If it was because of something you did or did not do, they should tell it to you as a matter of ethics. If they still refuse, you should seek the advice of a lawyer, but don't tell them about that during the meeting—or even afterward. Don't do anything to further weaken or prejudice your position.

START NEGOTIATING
IMMEDIATELY

9

It would seem that when a company fires an employee there are no options to get a better deal. Yet severance packages are commonly negotiated all the time. A reasonable severance package can neutralize employee anger and forestall possible legal action.

Most people have a good (healthy) self-image and put themselves in the "white hat" category of the good guys. Even thorough-going villains rationalize their villainy as someone else's fault: "It's a dirty job, but someone's got to do it." They'd like to think they at least treated you with kindness, even generosity, despite having had to fire you. In small companies it's usually the top man who does the firing, but in larger companies the task is often assigned to someone on a lower level of management, perhaps from the personnel department, who may not be very enthusiastic about delivering the news.

As a matter of fact, unless the person firing you is the office sadist or dislikes you, the task of firing you will be repugnant. Firing an employee means that from now on, until she finds another job, she will have no means of support other than unemployment checks. Her career will be dealt a blow, and there will be a gap in her résumé to explain away. Her spouse, children, elderly parents, and everyone else depending on her will suffer until she finds another job. This is not an assignment that a thoughtful, sensitive, and considerate person discharges with enthusiasm. If you're able to get safely past the act of being fired, you may be able to take advantage of the situation to your benefit.*

It is vitally important that you negotiate your terms before you're out the door—either when you find out in advance what's coming, or when it actually happens. Your ex-employer will become less and less cooperative in granting your requests the longer you are gone and you lose important bargaining leverage as time slips by. While you're still employed, the company has a responsibility to treat you equitably, to ease you out the door in a manner calculated to least harm the company, or you. After you are no longer an employee you become the enemy, or at the very least someone who can no longer help the company—and who may be in a position to harm it.

Many employers are now amenable to more generous severance negotiations than they once were. The higher up the corporate ladder you go, the more generous the package becomes. Many companies offer attractive early retirement plans as alternatives to firing. Those who refuse the packages run the risk of being fired. If your company offers you a reasonably decent package, you must realize that, should you refuse, you are probably at risk. However, don't assume that your employer is going to offer you a severance package unless it was part of your deal when they hired you, or you are a top executive, or they fear repercussions from you for any reason. If you go away quietly, they will breathe a sigh of relief because they got rid of you without having to pay anything for it. It's

---

*Warning: *Don't sign any document given to you by your employer at this time until you have had a chance to think it over, show it to your advisors, and evaluate it, especially if it's a condition of your severance package. It may seem logical at the moment, but you might be signing away some rights you'll need later. Take the document politely, put it in your pocket, and tell them that you will respond tomorrow or next week. You don't want to foreclose any options by signing a document that, for example, waives all claims against the company by you, now or in future.* Don't sign anything, *no matter how innocent-appearing, unless you have studied the contents. Consult an attorney if you don't understand the document.*

up to you to raise the issue and the ante, and do it at the time of your firing.

A full listing of all the legal ramifications—what the law says you may or may not be entitled to—and help available in each state by public and private institutions is beyond the scope of this book. Fortunately, there are several excellent guides devoted solely to your legal rights and entitlements as a result of being fired, written in nontechnical language by labor attorneys and others. One of your first stops after you are fired should be the business section of your local library or bookstore. If you decide to quit before you are fired, do your homework: Study your situation in books on the subject such as this one and visit your state's human resources (unemployment) office to learn your rights. If indicated, it might be worthwhile to buy an hour's worth of time from a good labor lawyer. It could save you money in the long run. The government has passed laws concerning severance agreements. Learn your rights before you need to use them, so that if and when you are fired, you'll be prepared to negotiate a fair severance.

It's important to look into this in some detail, preferably before the need arises. For example, if you have been putting around $2,000 per year into a 401(k) plan in which you will be fully vested in five years, and there are only a few months left before it is vested, or even an entire year, it may be worth waiting out the period if you can, so you can get your employer's contribution and thereby double your money when you draw it out. You can rationalize a much longer wait than that to collect an extra ten thousand dollars at the end of it. That's worth putting up with your job for a little longer.

Here are some important issues to negotiate:

1. *Severance Pay:* * Don't ask your employer how much money you may expect. Your advance research should give you an idea

---

Severance pay should ideally be paid to you in full upon leaving. Some companies may want to pay it only until you get your next job. This is not acceptable because then the severance becomes the equivalent of salary and may disqualify you from collecting unemployment insurance until it's gone. Also, by paying it out over a period of time, the company can use it as an implied threat, in case you decide to appeal your firing. It is ethical and usually customary to pay severance in full at the time of parting. If your former employer insists, you may wish to consult the labor board or an attorney for an opinion on how to proceed. If it is company policy to pay it out over time, you may be forced to accept this method. But be sure to get a letter from an officer of the firm stating that it is severance pay. If you get it all in one lump payment, bank it immediately and don't touch the money unless you have to for ongoing expenses. Ration it like water in the desert, for that's what it is.

what others have received, so you can estimate what you consider fair. Without being confrontational, tell your employer you understand that you had to be fired and that the company has a reputation for fairness, so you feel that he will be fair with you; therefore you expect "X" weeks of severance pay based on "X" years with the company, your good record, etc. Bring up any reasons you may have for increasing this amount. You may have been responsible for the firm's getting an important client or contract; you may have an excellent attendance record or have received achievement awards for meeting goals. Most people want to do the right thing. It will help them justify firing you if they can claim later that they bent over backward to treat you well. Whatever you have to offer, offer it now to support your claim for a larger settlement. Once you have taken the initiative by stating your expectations before your employer has had a chance to tell you what, if any, severance he had in mind, you have drawn a line. Your severance pay plus unemployment benefits will become your budget, your salary, and your expense account until you get another job. That is why it's critical to get as much as you can. Eighty-three percent of all companies give severance pay to fired or laid-off employees even though they are not required to. This indicates a sense of obligation to make the parting more palatable for the employee and at the same time salve the conscience of the employer. It's also a way to forestall possible legal action by the unhappy ex-employee. There is no rule, although the custom is to offer one or two weeks of pay for each year worked. Of all the issues to negotiate, this is the most flexible area between employer and employee. Try to find out your company's policy before you are fired (preferably soon after you are hired) by asking around discreetly. (You don't want to give management any ideas!) Only around 60 percent of companies have severance policies, and it's not usually found in the company manual. This allows each case to be handled on its merits—besides, management doesn't want you to be thinking of leaving just as you have been hired.

2. *More Severance:* Negotiations don't have to be concluded in one session. Even if you and your (former) employer have both agreed on a figure, you still might try for a bit more. You aren't begging, or "stooping to their level." Don't let false pride guide you here. You

are negotiating for your survival until you can get another income stream started in your next job, so go for it! Come back the next day and tell him that you ran the figures and, even though the offer was reasonable, you will have a hard time unless you can get a little more. Analyze your position and use whatever reasons you legitimately have to get a bit more from the company. If you're in the forty-something age group, mention how hard it is for people your age to find work in these times. If you have a family at home that depends on you, be sure to speak about them. Appeal to your employer's sense of fair play, and work on his emotions as well as his logic: guilt, the desire to avoid publicity, to just get rid of you, the urge most people have to be fair. The company's representative may take a hard-line position and tell you the figure is firm, take it or leave it! Consider going over the head of this person. Go directly to the president of the company, if you feel the situation calls for a higher authority. Remember, you've already been fired. The worst thing they can do to you now is say no. If they have any decency, they will try to bend over backward to satisfy your reasonable demands and have you leave satisfied.

If all else fails, you can use the services of a lawyer to help, although you should never threaten this in your negotiations. Once that threat has been made there will be a vast change of attitudes. Now the company will need to be defensive and noncommittal on further concessions, and you may find that the meeting is suddenly over. You may have to sue in the end, or file a complaint with the labor board, but you can do that later. No one can state for certain how far to push, and all situations are different. But you will shortly be out on the street. This is your last chance to get a better deal, so give it your best effort. If you're in shock from the firing and simply walk away, you may be missing a chance to better your situation. Many times you can negotiate a few more weeks or months of pay by making your case. At this time, when emotions are high on both sides, your employer is more likely to concede than afterward, when passions have cooled.* This is not

---

*You're not required to accept your employer's severance offer (or any other aspect of the severance package) at this time. It is permissible, and acceptable, to say that you need time to think. This allows you to re-analyze your strategy, talk it over with a wiser person, decide to accept or reject the offer, and go back a day or so later and reopen the subject. Maybe your employer has had a change of heart by then. Time can be your friend, so don't hurry.

the time for false pride. No one is watching how you behave except the person firing you and yourself. Whatever your attitudes may be about bargaining in general, disabuse yourself of them at this time. What you get now is all you will have until you're once again employed, and you have no idea how long that will be, or at what salary level and what the benefit package will be in your next position. *Always, always, always ask for more severance pay,* no matter how generous the company's offer seems. They can only say one of two things: yes or no. Visualize how much money your company wastes on what you consider nonsense or unnecessary expenses, and then tell yourself that what you're asking for is vitally necessary.

3. *Your Severance Terms in Writing:* Ask your employer to put in writing that it is severance pay and not salary because you won't be able to collect unemployment benefits until all salary has been used up.[†] (Check this out with your state's unemployment insurance office.) Severance pay is not considered salary in most states. You should get in writing all other aspects of your severance package for your records. This will prevent the "I never said that" syndrome from arising on either side.

4. *Other Monies You May Be Owed:* If you have accumulated vacation or sick leave, ask to have it converted into cash. Many companies offer outplacement services to laid-off or fired employees.[††] These services cost the company money, so it's not unreasonable to ask for the cash equivalent if you don't intend to use the service. Before you make this request, however, take a look at outplacement and see if you want it. A good outplacement service will counsel you on where your career is going and help you to analyze your strengths and weaknesses, seeking the best

---

[†] *When you have completed your negotiations, summarize them in a letter and ask your employer to sign one copy. Or have her write the letter and you both sign. Passions cool and people change their minds. Avoid problems later by getting it in writing. If your employer is a reasonable person she'll understand and will want the letter as well to protect the firm from further demands from you.*

[††] *"Laid off" implies that there is the possibility of being rehired, should conditions improve. While this is often a euphemism for being fired, it's a gentler way of putting it. While it is possible to be rehired after being fired, the latter term implies finality with no recourse.*

type of job or career for you. Many fired employees have been helped not only to find another job, but also to make strategic decisions about where they're going with their professional lives. Another potential for additional money is your annual bonus, if your firm gives them. Had you not been fired you might have expected one this year as well. You worked hard; perhaps they would consider prorating your bonus from January first to the day you leave. These are all gray areas. Companies are not required to give cash equivalents, but many do in an attempt to treat the employee fairly and professionally. Saying no to your request may induce the company to give you a concession in another part of the severance package that you are asking for. Ask! Ask! Ask!

5. *Letter of Reference:* You are now unemployed and have a problem. You've just been fired and are going back into the job market with a negative mark to explain to prospective employers. It would be helpful if you could produce a letter of reference describing your good record with the company, achievements, personal recommendations ("gets along well," "a team member," etc.). The letter should state the reason you are being let go.

The time to get the letter of reference is now, before you're gone and passions have cooled. Joan R.'s immediate superior harassed her. Appeals to senior executives were unavailing, and she didn't want to pursue the matter in the courts. She resigned instead. She was promised a letter of reference but didn't press the issue. A few weeks later her former employers were telling everyone that she was a troublemaker and was asked to quit.

When she applied for unemployment insurance, it was refused because of the company's misrepresentation of the reason for her departure. She requested an administrative review (remember that term, you may need it) and the lower judgment was overturned in her favor, allowing her to qualify for unemployment insurance and exposing the company's duplicity.

She never did get her letter of reference, but she might have if she had presented her employers with a draft of one while still employed. The letter would have made the resulting unpleasantness moot. If your boss is a lowlife and refuses your request, go over his head to his boss or the president of the company, if you can. If you cannot get one from an officer of the firm, try your department head. Unless you're being fired for a major transgression, there should be no objection. Failing this, try to get letters of recommendation from clients, even suppliers. Sure, you can tell prospective employers that you have a letter of reference from your former employer and may never be asked to produce it. But if you say that, you'd better have the letter with you. Also, get character references from people whose reputations are respected. Even if you have an employer's letter of reference, it helps to have good character references also. Letters are best, but character references may take the form of a listing on your résumé, implying that prospective employers may check them out (they probably will). Always ask for permission to use someone's name as a reference. If the answer is yes, ask for a "To Whom It May Concern" letter from them to use in your job-seeking efforts.*

6. *Miscellaneous Requests:* If you drive a company car, ask to keep it until you get another job. If the company has registered you in a country club or a health gym, ask to continue with it until the next job. These perks may not be necessary but are nice to have. What other company benefits do you get that might be worth holding onto for a while, if the company agrees?

Other Considerations Before Leaving

Many companies offer individual and family counseling to those who are fired. Also offered in many cases are services to help the employee get another job, sometimes even in a division of the same company. If you have need of these services, use them (unless you traded them for

---

In the present litigious atmosphere of corporate America, many companies are increasingly reluctant to give references to ex-employees. This often extends to a refusal to give out information to prospective employers who may call to check up on someone they want to hire. The former employers fear lawsuits, and the phrase "disgruntled employee" strikes terror in some corporate boardrooms. As a result, references have become problematical of late and employers are increasingly relying on their own judgment and on the prospective employee's résumé and supporting documentation. This works to your advantage by putting your presentation to future employers higher on the decision-making process than before. To play it safe, many companies only verify that the ex-employee did indeed work for the firm and the dates of employment.

more severance pay). Don't let your emotions take over here. The emotional toll on the person being fired and her family, especially children, can be devastating. Counseling often softens the blow and makes it understandable. You will need a new job right away and the employment counselor your firm uses may just be the one who helps you find it. You need all the help you can get in this trying time. Don't let foolish pride become your phantom enemy—you have enough problems already.

Cleaning Out Your Desk

It's a bittersweet job and can bring tears to your eyes, this business of cleaning out your desk. You may be tempted to hold on to all the little souvenirs of trade shows and conventions, employee luncheons, and office parties for the memories of friendships and good times they bring. But along with the calendars and the magnets, the plastic globe of the world, the potted plant, and all the rest of the odds and ends that make up most people's desk leavings, are some things that are important to take.

If you can't take the Rolodex file, at least copy out the information or photocopy it. Your job search could start with this. It's the single most important thing you need as you head out the door, as we shall see later. It contains the names and phone numbers of the people you'll want to call to tell them the news and to ask them for help in finding another job. Take all the files that belong to you and any personal property. Don't take anything else.

You may be seething inside, but you must not show your anger by your expression or what you say. Time has a way of turning the world upside down, and those people you're saying good-bye to may be the ones you need in the future. A cynical sign I saw in someone's office once said, "Be nice to people you pass on the way up . . . you might meet them on the way down!" It's important for your self-respect, if for no other reason, to maintain as much emotional equilibrium (grace under fire) as possible, and if you can't muster a cheerful expression, at least don't go around muttering darkly and scowling. Go for a walk around the block, and when you return, take time to visit all your colleagues to say good-bye and thank them for all the help they gave while you worked there. Be sure to get their home phone numbers—you may want to invite them to your party when you get the new job that's waiting out there for you. They can also be a source of leads for your next position.

Your final act—are you up to it?—should be a visit to your boss to say good-bye. Unless your parting was acrimonious there's no reason why you can't be civilized, even if he wasn't. You're not forgiving him—it's too soon for that. All you are doing is being decent. You owe it to yourself. Think of it as the start of the healing process. Don't get into negative discussions with anyone you say good-bye to, especially the boss! This is no time for sour grapes. Tell them how much you enjoyed working with them, that you'll miss them (if that's the truth), and that you hope to see them again.

Walk out with your head up and a smile on your face. The rest of your life is waiting outside.

Survivor Guilt

Management is beginning to realize that wholesale firings can demoralize an entire company. Even one or two firings affect the performance of those who remain. This can result in lower productivity, carelessness (with possible job-related accidents), absenteeism, pilferage, and a more sympathetic ear to union organizers.

It may come as small comfort to learn that those who are not fired, whose jobs for the moment are safe, will also suffer from your firing. Those left behind often feel akin to the survivors of an accident who feel guilty because they were spared while others perished, or the feelings of soldiers who watched their comrades die on the battlefield and then felt guilty because they were still alive.

Two Boston psychologists, Dr. Gloria Spitalny and Dr. Stuart Clayman, have identified what they call post-downsizing stress disorder, or PDSD. Among the symptoms of PDSD, according to Drs. Spitalny and Clayman, are the aforementioned survivor guilt, anger about doing the job of those who left in addition to one's own job, isolation, termination phobia, depression, concentration problems, performance anxiety, and physiological symptoms such as headaches and upset stomachs—not exactly a good recipe for building employee morale and team spirit.

Dr. Spitalny was first made aware of the phenomenon when a senior executive of a company called her one day. Someone had been fired and the remaining staff was in an uproar. While the CEO, unaware, labored blissfully away at his problems in his office, the staff, like an orchestra gone mad, were all playing a different song. The person fired, a woman who had been doing what she, and others, thought was a good job, was approached by her supervisor, told that she was fired, and given one hour to clear out of the office. Her nightmare started there, but so did another, different nightmare for everyone else left behind. The message they got was: If this employee, an honest, good person, couldn't be trusted, then everyone else in the company must also be under suspicion. Once Pandora's box was opened, not only was the fired employee damaged, but everyone else in the company was affected, including the supervisor who did the firing. It turned out that she had never fired anyone before and was wracked with guilt for what she had done. How the company handles firings from the corporate end often serves the company ill and does more damage than good.

So widespread has the phenomenon become in this age of downsizing that there is a National Anxiety Screening Day, now in its third year, and held (with no irony intended) on Labor Day, September first, the day set aside by Congress to honor the workers of the land. If you think you suffer from PDSD, you can find out more about it by contacting Powersizing Consulting Company, 416 Commonwealth Avenue, Suite 607, Boston, MA 02215 (telephone 617/266-0422). If you use the Internet, go to http://www.cybercom.net/~gloria/stress.html/ and take their free stress test.

AFTER THE FIRING . . . NOW WHAT?

You managed to get through the firing without going to pieces. Now it's over and you're out on the street. You took your photos off the wall of your workstation and put a few belongings in your pocket or purse and will come back tomorrow to take the rest of whatever belongs to you.*

Get the Facts Down Right Away

But before you let off steam and begin the grieving process for your deceased job, you still have one or two things to do, right

---

* There may be an urge to take more than is yours. You are not displaying weakness of character. Nor have you suddenly turned into a criminal. This is a normal desire to wreak at least a little revenge, to "show them." Resist it! You are not a thief and stealing is illegal. Leave crime to professional criminals.

now! Go home, take a pad, and while the details are still fresh, *write down everything that happened during and immediately after the firing.* Date the paper and sign it. Put down details like the time of day you were fired, who was present, the name and position of the person who fired you, the reasons given, and as much of the conversation as you can remember.

This serves two important purposes:

1. In the event you decide to take legal action, you'll need a complete record to build your case. If you write it down now, while you remember everything, it will have the urgency and wealth of detail needed to be a valuable exhibit. As time goes by you forget the details that lend credence to an account written right away. Judges place great weight on diaries, journals, and other documents written at the time of the incident. No matter how you may wish to forget the ugly episode, even if you are not now contemplating legal action, write it down.

2. Writing it out makes you feel better. Firing creates a chaotic state of mind. Your predictable world of nine to five is gone. You no longer have a place to go to in the morning. Nor do you have a salary. You need to bring some semblance of order back to your life, and the best way to start is to write down everything that happened just now. Many professional writers claim that writing is therapy, the cheapest and maybe the best. By writing it down you find yourself explaining to yourself what happened. Your subconscious then goes to work sorting things out and making it emotionally manageable by objectifying it. Psychoanalysis is basically the recollection and reliving of experience in an attempt to make sense of it. Most religions have a structured technique for confiding to someone what is troublesome. What is praying but the relating of events and a call for help?

Talking to Yourself

People who talk to themselves seem odd, especially if the talking is accompanied by shouts and violent gestures. But writing on a piece of paper is a form of talking to yourself, as is sitting quietly in your room and thinking out loud. Writing a poem or short story, or a bit of country and western music, are forms of talking to oneself, or thinking out loud. Even writing a full-length novel can be a form of self-therapy—the author as therapist and client, all at once. Talking to someone with a sympathetic ear, like a spouse or close friend, can be akin to talking to yourself. There's nothing wrong with it in the aftermath of a traumatic incident like being fired. It's a safe way of letting off steam and explaining what happened to the most important person in the world . . . you!

Elizabeth Kubler-Ross, the renowned death therapist, wrote about the process of grieving as it relates to the loss of a loved one. Getting fired is analogous to dying. Your job—a piece of yourself—has been executed. Up to now, you went to work each day and were paid to do certain tasks in which you (mostly) took some pride. Suddenly, all that was yanked out from under you, and you were cast out, to make your way in the world. Your job is dead. Finished! No more will you go to "work" each day, and be paid for your labor.

You carry this half-death inside your still-living body, and you just don't know how to handle it. The steps to healing are similar to what you go through after the death of a loved one. At first you are in denial: "I don't believe this is happening to me!" Then comes sorrow: "My beautiful job is gone. I will never again see the happiness I knew at the firm." Then comes anger: "I'll show them. How dare they?" and so on. You feel like Hamlet plotting revenge against his uncle. Finally comes acceptance. At this point you are ready to get another job. The hurt of your loss will remain with you for a long time, perhaps years, perhaps forever. The injustice of it all! The cruelty and unthinking brutality of how they did it! But the longer you dwell on it, the unhealthier it gets. Shake it off, pick yourself up, and move on. You will do many happy things yet with your life and will eventually fulfill your destiny, but only if you throw this experience off and put it behind you.

Your task (your "work" now) is to do this exorcism as rapidly as possible. What happened happened—and that's that! Now, start the rest of your life. Today! If you're still so upset that you need more than a few days to get over it, perhaps you need professional help or at least a heart-to-heart talk with a good friend or advisor. Or maybe a little vacation, a change of scenery for a few days or a week, will do the trick. But the most effective therapy is a new and better job. Success is the best revenge. The sooner you buckle down and concentrate on your job search, the sooner you will heal completely.

Start now by talking to yourself, as it were, on paper, where you will relive the event in order to get it down right. Once you've completed this painful step you'll feel better. The healing will have begun.

While you have your pad out, there are a few more writing chores you need to do before the event cools and memory erases important facts. List all the friends and colleagues, neighbors, and acquaintances you know who could possibly help you as you go out to search for a new job. It's important to list all of them. It's amazing who knows who in this world. Your barber or hairdresser might have a client whose business needs someone just like you. Your travel agent knows dozens of people. One of them might have the key to your future. It's called networking, and it means "working the net." Make your net as large as you can, and get to work on it right away. You'll need to tell the world that you are available, and you'll need to keep at it until you are once again employed. We'll have more to say about networking later.

How Long Will You Be Out of Work?

The lucky ones waltz into another job within a week or two. Don't you count on it. You will be out of work anywhere from a month to a year, and in rare cases even longer. It depends on many variables, such as the conditions in your industry or trade, the part of the country you live in, the state of the economy locally, nationally, even internationally, and other factors. If you look assiduously for three or four months and come up with nothing, you'll have to make some hard decisions. Are you in the right place to find work? Should you consider changing careers into something more in demand than your last job? Should you take the plunge and go into business?

Whatever your period of unemployment turns out to be, take control of your job search by setting time limits. You cannot predict or dictate when you will get another job, but you can set limits, now! Two to three months is a reasonable time in which to locate and get another job. The realities of life will undoubtedly stretch it farther, but don't let that stop you from trying to control what now seems uncontrollable. Setting tight limits will do many things for you. It gives you a time frame within which to operate, creates the sense of urgency that your condition needs, and will probably result in your being out of work for a shorter period than if you don't. It also gives you the feeling that you are in control of your destiny to the degree you can be, under the circumstances.

Your reasons for wanting a job quickly should be obvious. You need to get another income stream going and get on with your life without suffering the traumas that having no money in the pocket leaves in its wake. You also don't want to present the illusion of unemployability to prospective employers. There is no shame in being out of work, although that's hard to swallow in a country that takes great pride in its work ethic and boasts the highest productivity in the world. We Americans are workers and proud of it, and we tend to look at people who are out of work a bit oddly. "Why, if they'd only pull up their socks and get out there, they'd find a job!" we think subconsciously. This attitude permeates our professional lives as well. If you are out of work for a long time, prospective employers will wonder why, even if they know that conditions in your industry are bad and a lot of people are out looking.

That's a compelling reason to get back to work quickly and why you need to set short term limits on how long you expect to be out of work. The reality of life in America today is that you may be looking at a long, hard road stretching many months ahead before you arrive at the door of your new employment and walk in. Everybody knows that, but "everybody" is human, too, and can't help but wonder . . . .

Employment counselors vary widely in how long they think someone should be out of work, which is probably an accurate reflection of a question that has a hundred answers, all of them right and all of them wrong to some degree. There are so many variables—such as conditions in the industry, availability of jobs in a geographic area, your personal story—that no prediction can hold for everyone. If you have been working for a long time it may come as a shock to learn that salary levels have gone down in many industries, along with employee benefits once taken for granted.

If you are in an afflicted industry you may have to take a job at a lower salary level than you expected. This contradicts the American dream which, if it ever really existed, assumed that each job was a step up on the great upward-mobility ladder and that salaries gradually increase until retirement. Whether or not you should resign yourself to expecting a lower salary, or asking for somewhat more than you got on the last job, is impossible to answer without knowing all the facts in your case. Do a quick salary survey of your field. This can involve a visit to the library or simply some phone calls to friends in the business for their views. Read the want ads to get some idea of salary levels or talk frankly with a job counselor or executive recruiter that you may know or are using in your job search.

You are not changing jobs as a career move. You're seeking a job because you have been fired. While that's nothing to be ashamed of, it puts you at a tactical disadvantage: You need to get *them* to hire *you*. They are not seeking you out. The subject of having been fired is white hot in your head, but it may not even occur to those you apply to that you have been fired. It's a subtle difference in attitude, but, if you're still smarting about it, it could affect your attitude and how you present yourself. While you shouldn't lie (they'll check anyhow), you should lower in importance the issue of your firing. It's history. If you were fired because of impersonal conditions beyond anyone's control (the company closed a division, for example), state it simply if asked and get on to something else.

Should You Sue the Bastards?

Your second step, if you think your firing unjust, should be to head to a lawyer's office. This does not commit you to making a case against your former employers. But you owe it to yourself to know your rights. While legal action may not be indicated or even desirable, there is a huge and growing body of law governing the firing of employees. Go to your state department of labor or a labor specialist attorney. If you don't know any, call the local bar association for a list of names and talk to a few on the phone before you decide whom to visit. Consider the fee for an hour of your lawyer's time as an investment in yourself. As you would go to a doctor if you don't feel well, you should go to an attorney when your legal rights don't feel well, and right now they're a bit rocky.

One final note before you go out into the storm. Jobs, like divorces, can sometimes be reconciled. If you left on relatively good terms and no bridges were burned—if you liked your job and your employers liked you and approved of the job you did, firing you only because they had to—there is often a possibility that you might be rehired in the future. Maybe you were fired because of industry conditions or because the company lost a major account through no fault of yours and can no longer afford to maintain your position. Perhaps the manager who ordered your firing will leave the company soon, thereby removing a possible objection to your rehire. There are a hundred reasons why you may have been let go and, in some cases, you may be eligible for rehire.

Albert S. was given early retirement from the large corporation he worked for as a vice president, ending a distinguished career. Corporate changes dictated the move, one which he was not in favor of at the time. While early forced retirement is not exactly like being fired, it's tantamount to the same thing. His company thereupon contracted with him as a part-time consultant when they found that they still had need of the special knowledge he had. He now works for them on a project basis and for the last two years has made more money and is working fewer hours than when he was a full-time employee.

It's always wiser not to burn your bridges behind you, tempting though it may seem at the time.

Can You Survive Financially?

Do a quick statement of net worth. The purpose of this exercise is to let yourself know exactly what your resources are and how long you can afford to be out of work. Make a budget based on how much money you have and how long you expect to be out of work (one year is a conservative estimate). But before you do your own budget, as an exercise in objectivity do a dry run. Assume that you are someone working in a low-paying job with a survival salary, say, $15,000 a year. Make out a budget for this imaginary person, how much they may spend on the necessities of life, and be sure that it comes in under the total. If the figure above sounds unrealistic to you, raise it to what you consider the right level, but be sure that it's still a low survival level. This exercise will bring the problems you face clearly to the fore and is good preparation for the real budget, which you will now do.

Taking the amount of money you have on hand, divide it into twelve portions, one for each month you expect to be out of work. Then run the budget, laying in all the fixed expenses that must be paid to keep things afloat. This will tell you what moves you need to make and where you need to conserve money. It might dictate the necessity of selling your car for a cheaper model or moving to a smaller apartment, or taking a loan. The problems are all similar, but the solutions for each person will be different, which is why you must do a budget for your particular situation.

"Use it up, wear it out, make it do, or do without." That slogan adorned thousands of posters on the home front during World War II, when shortages plagued the civilian population. It's not a bad slogan for one who is out of work and doesn't have an income anymore, either. You are really on what was then called a war footing. Think of ways you can save money. With a little imagination and sacrifice you can save significant money without seriously crippling your lifestyle. For example, watch movies on television or rent videotapes instead of going to the theater. Wash your own car instead of going to the car wash. Clean your apartment once a week yourself instead of hiring a cleaning person. Do your own ironing.

Your weekend newspaper has listings of free lectures, concerts, and performances. Most museums have a free day once a week or a few times a month. Get reacquainted with your library and its collections. You'll find all sorts of wonderful things available free (or nearly so) in your community that will prove entertaining, educational, and uplifting. You may find all sorts of facilities in your neighborhood that you may never have known about but for this temporary setback. Many of them can enrich your life and widen your horizons.

Most people who have worked for a time have at least a little money saved. If you have some savings but not enough, it's time to make a budget. List all your fixed expenses, such as utilities, rent, estimated food costs for a month, laundry and dry cleaning (you'll probably need more than usual for job interviews), car or bus fares, loan payments, insurance payments, and all the other expenses you absolutely have to make, month by month.

Then inventory your savings and any other sources of money you may have. If you invested in stocks or mutual funds, consider the possibility of cashing in all or part of them. But don't do it until you absolutely must. You may get a job sooner than you think and then regret any hasty action. If you have a new or late-model car, it might be wise to consider selling it and getting a transportation vehicle, at least until you're back on salary. This could be the answer to the problem for many people, allowing enough cash from the sale to buy a cheaper car with enough money left over for many months on a tight budget. It also gets rid of your car-loan payments.

When you have listed all your fixed expenses, add another ten percent for safety, and project the budget for a year by multiplying by twelve months. You'll probably get a job much sooner than that, but you must be prepared for the worst-case scenario. By subtracting your savings and other sources of money you will quickly know if you're in trouble. If you have only enough money to survive for six months, or four, you may want to take a chance on getting a job within that period, but it's a risky assumption.

Now is the time to make hard decisions such as selling your car. Riding the bus or subway can save a lot of money that you will need for other things. You can lower your rent by moving to a less expensive apartment, or moving in with a friend or your parents. Forget the emotional baggage that that last thought brings. If your relationship with your parents is good, they may want to help. You should not feel false pride. Robert Frost said that family are people who, when you come to them, have to take you in. If you do move in with them for a while, realize that they are different people now from the young and vigorous people who raised you. Respect their privacy, and do what you can to make your stay easier on them. They will appreciate your consideration.

Should you borrow money or take out a formal loan? This is a last-resort option, but one you must consider along with all the others. If you're confident of getting a job soon, you might try to get a larger line of credit on your credit card. Bank loans for this purpose are almost impossible to get, but, then, there are your parents to consider, if they have the money. This is always a tricky emotional route. If you borrow from family or friends, give them a written letter with your signature, telling the amount loaned, the date borrowed, and when and how you intend to repay it. Once you have your job, begin to faithfully repay such loans. It's a test of your character that you meet this obligation. If you don't, the consequences aren't worth it. Not only is your relationship with those you borrowed from at stake, but your self-image—your fundamental character as a moral, honest person—is at stake. Don't take it lightly.

ARE YOU A FAILURE?

Nothing succeeds like failure.

—Eugen Weber, KCET Broadcast

Unless your firing was due to circumstances beyond your control such as the elimination of a department, the loss of a contract that you were not personally responsible for, or some other impersonal reason, it's normal to feel that there is a failing, perhaps a character flaw in your psychological makeup, that led to your firing. Superstitious people believe that they are jinxed, born under the wrong sign, unlucky in life. If you believe this, you have a self-esteem problem. When people are fired, the first thing they naturally ask themselves is "Why?" If no logical and acceptable answer is forthcoming, the next question might be "Why me?"

A common reaction to being fired is guilt and shame. Most people equate having a steady job with being normal. We are indoctrinated from birth by our religions, our neighbors, our families, our culture, and our work ethic, which dictates that one must earn one's way in this world. Politicians get credibility from it—think of the mileage Harry Truman got from his Missouri haberdashery. So when we're fired it's perfectly normal to feel, at least at first, that there is something shameful, wrong, even sinful about it.

Why is this? As children, we did our chores in the household, brushed our teeth, took out the garbage, did our homework. In school we repeated the same formula in a more regimented way: going to school on time, leaving at the bell, and getting our milk and cookies, gold stars, and good report cards. (At least those of us who were lucky enough to have that kind of life.) From high school and college we moved seamlessly into the job environment—the "real" world—where we had more of the same. The boss became our parent and teacher substitute—we did our work and, instead of milk and cookies, we got raises and bonuses, promotions and vacations.

Then, one fine day, our parent/teacher/boss fired us! No matter what age we are, no matter how educated and mature we think we are, no matter how worldly our experience or sophisticated our personas—we failed momma, our teachers, our boss! We haven't just been deprived of dessert this time either, made to sit in the corner, exiled to our room, or grounded for a week—we have been bodily thrown out of the house we love, deprived forever of our parents, our family, our home, our very life structure. All because, somehow, we must have done something wrong. We have failed to meet their expectations. We are failures! What will we do now? Who will take pity on us and take care of us? We are orphans, now, alas.

Being fired is a rite of passage—an often necessary step we are pushed into that forces us to finally shed the womblike security of our job and go out into the world—and grow up, at long last. Firing is a loss of innocence. No more will we wonder what we really want to do with our life. We have to make that decision—and do it today! But we can't make the decision now—part of us has just died, and who can think clearly at a funeral? We must first finish grieving before we can think clearly about tomorrow.

Women, with their infinite ability to rationalize, seem to handle firings better than men, according to Dr. Gloria Spitalny, a Boston psychologist who specializes in work-related problems.* Men tend to identify themselves with their work, according to Dr. Spitalny. Their firing strips them of their identity, at least for a time.

Shame and embarrassment, left unchecked, will quickly develop into anxiety and from there it's only a short step to panic. That way lies confusion, wasted time, emotional damage, and perhaps even physical problems resulting from stress. More than one person, ashamed at being fired, has committed suicide.

If this book has tried to demonstrate one thing: Being fired, while not exactly an honor, is certainly far from a dishonor or anything that should be remotely connected to shame or guilt, *even if it's your fault that you were fired*—which in most cases it isn't. And it often results in positive things happening in one's life later on. Being fired is akin to a natural or man-made disaster. People are upset when there is a flood or a fire in their house, but no one is embarrassed by it. If there's any advantage to be gained from your experience it might be that, to paraphrase Samuel Johnson, it wonderfully clarifies the mind! He was referring to the sight of a noose, but the near-death of a firing will do as a substitute. Many people credit their firings as a wake-up call, a summons to concentrate on what's important, a loss of innocence but a gaining of maturity and a realization that in the end you have only yourself to rely upon. No savior will suddenly appear to turn your world into Technicolor, as Dorothy's was in *The Wizard of Oz*. Once you realize that not only will you not win the lottery, but that someone has just stolen your wallet, you begin to take charge of your life—and once you do that, you're on the way to success. (But as you begin to succeed, don't ignore the lottery completely. Chance favors us all, once in a while.)

If you have overwhelming feelings of embarrassment because you were fired, you may hide from your family and friends and waste a lot of time you should be using to get another job. If this describes you, the cure is to get out and talk to people, especially others who have been fired. Talk to your friends. If you belong to a church, synagogue, or mosque, talk to your religious counselor. Find out from him, or perhaps from your local mental health department, if counseling is available. Many churches and communities offer such assistance. Your ex-employer's

---

*See "Survivor Guilt" in chapter 9.

personnel department can give you a list of agencies where such counseling is offered.

Please read the previous paragraph over again. If you have *any* feelings of guilt or shame, you must overcome them before you do anything
else. Your mental and emotional health are crucial, not only to enable
you to get another job, but to deal with what happened, accept it, and get
back to normal again. Ask yourself how you will logically and convinc-
ingly explain to some future employer who wants to hire you that you
were fired if you go into the meeting feeling shame and guilt. You place
yourself in an impossible situation and dampen, if not eliminate, any
chance of presenting the facts acceptably. Thousands of people successfully get on with their lives all the time. Can you?

Give yourself the luxury of five minutes of self-pity—then banish those
thoughts! They will get you nowhere except into a depression, and that's
the last thing you need for a job search. There are only a few reasons to
fire someone. One: You committed an act so outrageous, blatant, or damaging as to require your removal. (If this describes your situation, then
you are fully aware of the reason for your firing and professions of ignorance are acts of denial.) Two: You lost your job for reasons that you may
suspect or that you possibly haven't the foggiest idea about, such as the
impending bankruptcy of your company, other corporate financial problems, market conditions, management's decision to downsize, or other
developments that require some digging up of facts to discover. Three:
You got in someone's way as he worked himself up the corporate ladder,
or you got on the wrong side of someone higher up, and because you are
lower on the totem pole, you got axed.[†]

If you can identify with the second or third reason and you still have
feelings of guilt and shame, you may need career or psychological counseling. Bill Sterling had a full-blown mid-life crisis when at age forty-two
he was fired as sales manager of an office machine wholesale distributor.
Bill was married and the only wage earner in the family. He had two teen-
age children, a mortgage, and other obligations and he was desperate.
His firing triggered a string of quasi-medical problems such as sleeplessness, stomach cramps, headaches, nervousness, and palpitations. He
became a chain smoker and developed a nervous tic. He was so distraught

---

[†]If that's the case, you may want to discuss the matter with an attorney.

that had it not been for the deep bond between him and his wife, it might have resulted in a separation.

Bill took advantage of his company's severance offer of professional counseling. After several months of therapy, he began to learn the truth about himself. He had always wanted to work with his hands, but because he felt it was his duty to be the breadwinner, to "get ahead," he went into sales rather than follow his urgings because he was convinced that sales was where the money was. He also suspected that people who worked with their hands were less highly regarded. During this time he outfitted a complete woodworking shop in his garage as a hobby to escape workaday boredom. He soon became a skilled furniture maker.

For twenty years he worked in sales and made a good, if unspectacular, living, paid his bills, and was a good husband and father. But he lived each day in anticipation of getting home at night, eating dinner, and working in his shop. He became a clock watcher. Bill was fired twice before in his sales career. This time, though, it got to him.

Bill's self-denial, the result of what he regarded as his sacrifice for his wife and children, led to a deep malaise whose outward symptom was an increasing lack of interest in his career, which slowly metamorphosed into a hatred of it. He turned this hatred inward and was well on the way to becoming an embittered man when he lost his job for the third time. Because of his growing lack of interest in office machine sales, his sales record declined and he began making mistakes in judgment. It did not go unnoticed and eventually led to a crisis that resulted in his firing.

Thanks to a skillful counselor and the encouragement of his wife, who took a job to help the family through the crisis, Bill made the decision to leave sales and try his luck with his first love: cabinetry and furniture making. Today he and his wife run a successful business making furniture to order and repairing and refinishing expensive antique furniture. His designs have won several awards and his work has been featured in several museum exhibits. His medical symptoms soon disappeared, and he quit smoking. He has developed a line of furniture-refinishing kits that are sold in hardware stores and says that in a few more years he will be able to retire. "But I don't intend to," he said to me *says*, grinning. "I'm having too much fun!" The career changing that is widespread in our society is largely due to the evolving nature of technology, manufacturing, and commerce. Bill's career change resulted from his being fired.

The poet Khalil Gibran wrote that the clay cup that holds the wine was first plunged into the heat of the oven before it could emerge in a beautiful and useful form.[1] "Failure is not something to be avoided. It is a natural and necessary part of life," says Wayne Allen Root, a motivational speaker.[2] Root failed in everything but clung to his dream, to be an anchor on a network sports show. He was told he had no talent, was unqualified, and was a joke. He had to act as his own agent because no agent would represent him. Root's object lesson was his father, who never traveled, never took a chance, and stayed with the job he hated because he was afraid of failure, afraid to try something different.

Not wanting to follow in his father's failed footsteps, Root never took no for an answer, sent out résumé after résumé until, finally, he broke through and achieved his dream. "You can be a victim, a survivor, or a thriver," he counsels; "it's a question of attitude."

HOW DOES MANAGEMENT EVALUATE EMPLOYEES?

12

If your company is small, the decision might be up to one or two people who, meeting informally, decide who gets promoted and who gets fired. Larger companies have more sophisticated methods. Employee relations specialists in large corporations are constantly evaluating each employee's performance, sometimes using methods that would be illegal outside the corporate environment such as eavesdropping, recording telephone conversations, reading employees' mail and computer screens, and using informers to spy on employees. They even announce their spying when you call and are put on hold: "In order to serve you better, this call may be monitored." Sure.

Most companies are fairly straightforward about evaluations and keep detailed records of each employee's progress. You may ask to see your record and in many cases the company will allow you to do so if you have a good reason. Many states, such as California, take the position that a terminated employee has the right to see her personnel file, even after she has left the company.[1] You may want to see if you can improve your job performance by finding company-identified problem areas. If your attitude is supportive, you may be permitted to see your record or have it summarized verbally for you. In such a meeting, be sensitive to eye contact (or lack thereof) and body language, as well as any verbal clues that might sound odd or problematical.

If your report indicates that you are an average employee, you're in trouble. When the time comes to fire people, it's the average employee who is in danger. The above-average employees are too valuable to fire (unless the company is in dire trouble), and those below average have either already been fired or were never hired in the first place.

Don't be lulled into complacency by a good report. Unless your employee record reads like the biography of Mother Teresa, it's only a guide. When the crunch comes, it may be ignored and pure emotion may dictate the decision. Sad to say, many people are fired on a whim.

Starting the Job Search Engine (The Customer Approach to Hiring)

Looking for a job is an odd business. There is no training for it, no school you can go to, like driver's training or accounting. You are not even completely certain what you're looking for or what you'll find, in many cases. And you operate under the handicap of "do or die." As a character in the movie *Apollo 13* said, "Failure is not an option."

Like the army private who was told he had just volunteered for a dangerous assignment, your firing thrust you into a fateful, involuntary mission. You don't have a moment to lose. Every day without a job is a day without a salary, another drain on your finances. Take a few days to get body and soul together. Maybe even take a short vacation. But as soon as you can, get to work on your mission. In your haste, though, allow enough time to plan your route. Decide if another job like the one you just left is for you or if you should try something different. You are making life-changing decisions that you'll have to live with for a long time, so be sure of yourself. Then go all out.

At this point you stand at a psychological fork in the road. You have three choices:

1. *Stand still and do nothing.* This is a form of mental paralysis, a holding of one's breath, hoping that this is a dream and that any second you'll wake up, back in your old job.

2. *Feel sorry for yourself.* Okay, a little of that is acceptable. But if you stay on that path you'll enter a nether world of unhappiness, misery, and emotional trauma that leads nowhere, except perhaps to a doctor's office, or worse.

3. *Take charge of your life again.* What does this old cliché really mean? In your case it means that you begin immediately to plan your escape from the purgatory of joblessness.

Taking Charge Again

When you were fired, you were knocked for a loop, blown away, dethroned. Before that, you arose each morning, punched in at work, put in your time and did your best for the company, punched out, enjoyed your evenings and weekends . . . lived a normal life, more or less. The firing not only removed you from your financial base but took away the structure you had grown accustomed to, the framework within which you lived your life.

Your task now is to innovate a framework within which you can "work," put up a tent, create a make-believe job, and take charge of that job in a regular, predictable manner. Your house or apartment becomes the tent because it is now less a symbol of your permanence and more a reminder of your transitory existence. The make-believe job is very real; it's your campaign to get another job. If you can visualize, or "picture" this campaign as a job, albeit without pay and without a corporate structure, you have made the leap of imagination that will make it possible to relax and concentrate on the "job" of getting a job. At this point you have your new framework and are in charge of your life once again. Most people go through this process unconsciously. If you can visualize it as described above, it will make your situation acceptable, emotionally and intellectually, at least for a while. The mainspring that will keep you going every day is the combination of the emotional and intellectual imperatives that will impel you out of bed in the morning and off to work—finding a job, perhaps today will be the day!

The first thing to do is look in the mirror. Are you overweight? Underweight? Do you look strained, relaxed? What does your hair, or lack thereof, look like? You are going to present that body you see in the mirror, costumed in your business finery, to total strangers and ask them to let you, your body, and your clothing, into their company to work there. Do you look like the kind of person someone would hire? Perhaps you need to lose a few pounds, get rid of the inner tube. You'll have time to do it now, and you certainly have the motive.

Inventory your clothes, have your car tuned, and get ready to go to work! Plan on visiting outplacement counselors, dozens of executive recruiters, or employment agencies, and plan on taking all sorts of tests for your aptitudes, skills, and education. Set goals. Plan to have your résumé done within the week. Plan to draft your first cover letter tomorrow. Plan to get references. You'll send out dozens, maybe hundreds of résumés—count on it. And each one with a cover letter. You'll make perhaps three to four hundred telephone calls before anything turns up. If you have a computer, you'll be surfing the Internet for jobs and related support services for hours, days on end. You'll construct mailing lists, and you'll be your own mailing department as you canvass your industry for a job.

The Fuller Brush Approach

Why all this action? The first reason: There's a lot of competition out there. The other reason is more prosaic but can be summed up with the phrase "changing the odds in your favor." The Fuller Brush man was once a fixture in many neighborhoods, going from door to door selling brushes. The salesmen were told that, in order to make one sale, you had to knock on ten doors. The eleventh would be your sale. Perhaps not in that order, but you get the idea. It could happen that the first job you apply for you'll get. But don't count on it, even as you pray for it to happen. You must raise the odds in your favor by generating dozens, hundreds, of leads, which will result in dozens of interviews. The more you work at it, the better your chances become. And the more you work at it, the more options you'll have to choose between jobs, so you don't have to take the first one that comes along.

The challenge you face is enormous and daunting, but you're up to it, never fear. You'll do it because you have no alternatives. You'll do it because you deserve a good job and are worth it. All you have to do is find that one person, in that one company, who will, finally, recognize that you're the best person for their job to walk through the corporate door since they started looking. It could happen tomorrow or, more likely, two months or more from now. But it will happen, bet on it!

Job Search Engines

First, a few definitions of terms—these are the resources and people who will help you get a job. We'll go into more detail farther on.

- *Employment Agencies:* These serve mainly entry-level jobs, or specialized jobs (chef, mechanic, teller, typist). They maintain a bank of available jobs and send applicants on interviews. They are paid by the employer, so if you're asked to pay a fee, use someone else. Because they fill the lower end of the job spectrum, their earnings depend on volume: the more jobs they fill, the more money they make. Getting sent out on interviews is easy, but sometimes you may find yourself applying for a job you don't want or aren't qualified for. Use them—they're free, after all—but remember, you're not their number-one priority.

- *Executive Recruiters:* As the name says, they recruit executives, in the $50,000-and-up category. Their services to you are also free, so use them freely. Send your résumé to as many as you can, without fear of duplication. The executive recruiters (commonly called headhunters) work on individual job assignments.*

- *Outplacement Services:* These are misnamed. They don't place you in anything, except maybe a desk, which you use to find yourself a job. What they do, and mostly do well, is become your backup team, your support group, and your advisers. They will help you decide what kind of job to get, advise you of the best way to get it,

---

*Answer all calls from executive recruiters, even if you're already working. First of all, you never know when the ax will fall on you in today's downsized environment. Second, they're the honeybees of employment. They know everybody and everything, and you can get valuable and useful information from them. They're worth cultivating. The caliber of their staffs are often quite high, and the best ones really want to help you get ahead.

help you with your résumé, and cheer you on when you're low. Many of them work for, or on references from, your ex-employer, some of which provide their services free as part of your severance package. Ask about them. They charge fees for their services but don't promise to find you a job.

- *Temporary Work Agencies (Temps):* These employment agencies traditionally supply companies with workers when the company's permanent employees are swamped, but management cannot justify hiring full-time employees. Money you earn while working for them affects your unemployment status, so research the options before you use them. Some companies often hire temporary employees for full-time positions. They're worth looking into if your skills are marketable to their core clients.

- *Networking:* This is your most powerful source of finding work, and it's all under your control! This is your network of friends, colleagues, and acquaintances whom you enlist in your job search.

- *Miscellaneous Resources:* These include the want ads in the papers and trade magazines, your local department of human resources (the old unemployment office with a new sign), your network of contacts, etc. We'll go into more details about these farther on.

The Job Search in a Nutshell

Every job search consists of three parts:

1. *Defining the job.* If you expect to be hired into a certain job, you must represent yourself clearly as a candidate for that job by training, experience, and desire. If you're not certain what kind of job you want, how can you expect anyone to hire you? If you cannot define what you want in one sentence, you should take a skills assessment test. There are many jobs that didn't exist only a few years ago and you may qualify for one of them, if only you knew what and where they are.

2. *Preparing the search tools (your credentials and résumé).* Getting a job is specialized work requiring specialized tools, such as a résumé, a network, and more.

3. *Selling yourself.* Once you have completed the first two steps, above, you have to actually go and get the job. It won't come looking for you, so you must find it, and sell potential employers the concept that you, and only you, are just the one they need for the job that's available.

How Much Will This Job Search Cost Me?

There's no easy answer to this question. It depends on how long you are out of work, how aggressively you search, how far afield you have to go. Industry wisdom says that for every ten thousand dollars of salary, figure a month out of work searching for the next job. This is a rule of thumb based on the concept that higher paying jobs are harder to get, and the selection process consequently takes longer. Factor in such variables as your age, industry conditions in the area and the rest of the country, and the status of the kind of job you want. That is, are there shortages of jobs in your field or is there a surplus of applicants? In the end, it's anybody's guess, and luck probably plays a part as well.

There are possible tax deductions involved in your search, so you should find out if, in your situation, it applies. Try the Internal Revenue Service or ask your accountant or whomever prepares your taxes each year. Like everything else in this confusing quest, there are gray areas. For example, if you're seeking a job that will advance your career, part of your expenses are probably tax deductible. On the other hand, if you're making a career change into something entirely different, they may not be. How the Internal Revenue Service comes to these conclusions is a mysterious process.

Play it safe and keep accurate records. If you have a doubtful expense, make the deduction and see if the IRS allows it. If they disallow it, you cannot deduct the expense, but, as in many IRS rulings, it's often a matter of interpretation. Get a large box and put every receipt you get into it after you have first entered the expense in a log. Use your computer to create an expense log in a spreadsheet program or a word processing program, or buy an expense account software program that will make it easy. If you don't use computers, get a ledger book from a stationery store and enter the date, what the expense was for, the amount, where purchased, and any other relevant information that supports your claim that it's a legitimate expense of job hunting.

Among the expenses to keep track of is car mileage going to job interviews, gas, tolls, parking fees, the occasional lunch you may have to buy someone, and all expenses relative to sending out résumés such as the cost of printing, postage, stationery, and business cards (even though you no longer have a job, you should have a business card to leave with people so they have a way of contacting you and remembering you). If you have to go out of town for an interview, keep track of expenses for the trip: airline fare or other transportation expenses, meals while out of town, hotel, etc.

If you use an executive recruiter to find a job you don't have to pay for this service. It's customary for the prospective employer to pay the recruiter's fee. If a recruiter demands a retainer or fee of any sort it's a tipoff that you're in the wrong place.

There is much emphasis on computers in this book.* Without one your job search will take longer and prove more expensive than it might otherwise be. For example, once you have the wording and layout of your résumé in your computer, you can print out only the number of résumés you need to apply for a job, whereas if you have it printed down at the local storefront print shop you'll need to place a minimum order of one hundred, or else have them photocopied, which looks inferior to a nice computer printout from a laser or inkjet printer on high-quality paper. You can also use the mail-merge capability of a computer to personalize a mass mailing of anywhere from six to six hundred job applications, each addressed to a different individual with personalized salutations.

You can tweak your résumé on a computer, slanting it for the particular job you're applying for, accenting what is needed and downplaying what is irrelevant. A computer-printed letter and résumé send the subtle and important message that you are computer literate and up to date with the latest technology. If you aren't a computer user yet, you should correct that immediately, especially now that you may have some spare time to devote to learning how to use it. Having a computer also

---

*Private organizations such as CompUSA, Egghead Software, and others offer concentrated basic and advanced computer training. Computer training is also generally available in many college extension courses and adult education evening classes, usually held in a local high school. The latter are often more time-consuming, while the former are more of the "crash course" variety. On the other hand, college extension courses usually more costly than the adult education classes.

gives you access to the Internet, where you just might find your next job.[†] Not being able to operate a computer has shifted from a show of independence to a display of stubbornness, fear, or ignorance and will not serve you well in today's business world.

Don't be reactive—be aggressive in your search. Nobody is going to come looking for you unless you have unique abilities. Answer all the advertisements and follow all the leads, but go further than that. Start scheduling interviews, not only for actual job opportunities, but with companies and people who may not have a position for you now but might in the future. You want to get on their list, get them to think of you when a need arises. Know the people there, make a good impression on them—and leave your résumé.

What Goes Around Comes Around

O. Henry, that wonderful author who specialized in surprise endings, would have loved this one. We retell it here because it reflects a basic truth often lost in the impersonal world that business has become. In her "At Work" column, Lindsey Novak tells the story of someone who learned about business from a boss who was, apparently, the soul of honesty, professionalism, and ethics. We'll arbitrarily call the employee a "she," although the story doesn't reference who it was. Nor is it necessary—the tale is universal.

She was reluctantly let go when her company was bought out and, with a generous severance package, went forth to find another job. Big shock! The recruiters and agencies she registered with treated her rudely, didn't return her telephone calls, and made her feel as if she was imposing on them. All this despite her ten years' banking experience plus a master's degree. She became miserable from the treatment and felt like a failure.

Then she was hired in the job of a lifetime, as the highly paid personnel director of a large bank. Guess who came calling? All the agencies and recruiters who had insulted and mistreated her while she was out of work and vulnerable—and whose business cards she had all carefully kept! They had clients for her to interview and wanted to set up appointments. She told each of them who she was and why she would not deal

---

[†]*See chapter 18, "Get Your Job on the Internet."*

with them. A few apologized, some hung up on her, while others sat in stunned silence.

The golden rule is named for the most precious metal in the world because it's so rare, so valuable, and so difficult to find.

The Employer Is Your Customer

When you are job hunting, getting hired seems as remote as a miracle. Fortunately for you, it turns out that you are a miracle-worker and a true believer. But everything seems so cold at first: your networking phone calls are not returned, potential employers seem disinterested, and blind ads you reply to don't respond. You begin to believe that getting hired is a cold and bloodless affair. It's nothing of the sort. It's the most human of activities, filled with moments of shining emotion and intelligence, as well as desperation and stupidity. True, management has many reasons to standardize the process: company policy, the need for them to maintain control, and their desire to avoid discrimination problems, to list a few.

All the rules in the world can only influence the results peripherally because hiring, in the end, is done by people: Real people with all their flaws and virtues, making decisions about your future—with incomplete information. People who are making a decision to ask you to fill a job—or to pass over you for someone else. People who want you to meet their needs. The people who do the hiring all have needs. Starting to sound familiar? It should. In the business world there's a name for people who have needs to be met. They're called *customers.*

The Customer Buys a Product

Step outside yourself for a minute and think of yourself as a product for sale. You need to be exactly the product the customer believes will satisfy his need. Getting hired does not mean that you will, or can, satisfy that need. That will be proven only after you're on the job. The customer, in buying your product (you), is acting like all customers: selecting from a variety of choices, making decisions on imperfect information, and wanting to believe in the correctness of his decision—that the product (you), will satisfy the need.

We are all customers, so we know what a typical customer wants. Let's look at the prospective employer as a typical customer and get some insights into how he will act in that role.

A typical customer scenario starts with a need. Let's say that your best pair of blue jeans are dirty and you need to clean them. You decide to buy some soap to clean your blue jeans. Down you go to your local market. There you're overwhelmed by the bewildering variety of soap products. Then you begin to make some sense out of the chaos. You examine the packaging. Patterns begin emerging. You're trying to make a selection from a variety of displays and signs all saying, in one way or another, "Soap . . . Plus."

You try to be thorough. From your examination of the claims on the boxes you select some products based on how well you believe, from the labels, that those products will meet your specific need. If there were a package that said "Great for Cleaning Blue Jeans," you would probably include that in your selection. If one says "Do Not Use to Clean Blue Jeans," it won't make the cut. After those easy choices, what other soaps might be included? You don't want to trust just one product, so you verify your decision with some backup.

The products by themselves don't know what your need is. They're only boxes of soap, presenting themselves through their packaging and labels, some specifically, some more generally. You know what you want, so if there is a product that promises to meet that need it will certainly be included for further consideration.

Now (help me out here, follow along and don't laugh!), if you were a box of soap, what would you want to do to make the cut, to be included in the next round? Products to be included must indicate that they will meet the need—that is, to show that in any review of soaps to clean your jeans they should not be excluded. Most of us would check the pricing first, after we make our initial choices from among the contenders. If the price is too high compared to the others, or too low, you won't include it with the group you've selected for further review. If the label offers so much extraneous information that one or more points hit the wrong chord, you would probably exclude it. If you couldn't figure the label out, that product stays on the shelf. The labeling must be designed and written to ensure that the product is not excluded.

Your next step would be sampling through use, or some approximation of use, to take the measure of the product. Sampling is just that—it approximates how the product will deliver its promises with long-term use. If you could, you'd buy a one-unit measure of each product and try them all out, testing them against your need, which only you know exactly.

In the process of selection and sampling, you discover that your need goes beyond merely cleaning your blue jeans. There are other clothes to be cleaned— that's another requirement. You found from your research at the market and your testing back home that a soap is available that leaves a nice odor after washing. Your need has expanded once again to include that. (Needs are not fixed—they grow and change as more options are recognized.)

Out of the sampling process comes a smaller group, as one after another product is discarded because it doesn't meet your needs. As you test the products, differences emerge. You eventually narrow your selection to two or three. From these you'll make your final purchase decision.

Maybe price now again becomes a consideration, but no longer the major consideration it might have been back when you were only reading labels. You are now selecting, after all, from products you like, all of which give promise of meeting your need. What are a few pennies, you muse, when your decision about something you are now beginning to believe will meet your need is to be made?

Recognize this process. Whether you call it the buying process or the hiring process, at its core there is simply another human being, a customer, making a choice to meet a need—to invest money in a product he has come to trust and believe in. Maybe the decision to buy takes longer, as you agonize over subtle differences, or maybe sooner, because your gut tells you it's right. You're the customer, and once you've made your decision about which product will meet your need, you will believe in that decision. You used all your powers to make it, and you'll defend that decision. You want your decision to be the right one, and you want everyone else to know that *it's the right decision.*

The only real test of the product is whether it actually fulfills—or even exceeds—your needs and expectations, but you won't know that for some time. And while that's the reason you think you made the decision, the real reason, as we have seen, is that the product successfully made it through all the steps in your exhaustive evaluation. The person hiring you goes through the same process, and in just as human a way.

Whatever a customer makes a decision about, those products that fulfill the requirements at each stage of the review are the ones with the best chance of being selected.

The best product, if it's presented in a plain paper bag, might not make it past the first cut. If first appearances aren't convincing, the fact that a product might be better over the long run will never be known. The "customer" who is going to hire you is going to act just like the customer in the supermarket. By following the steps, by meeting the customer's expectations at each stage, your product (you) will be the one that is bought (hired).

And you will be hired . . . with enthusiasm! Hiring is the most exciting win-win event in business: You win because you got the job and the hiring "customer" wins because his needs are met to his satisfaction—and perhaps, in your case, beyond.

The Customer Approach to Hiring

The customer is always right. That is your basis for this method of getting hired. Let the customer lead you and show you the way, right into your job. They know (or they *think* they know) what they want. You don't need to sell them—you just have to be sure that you're included at each of the customer's buying steps: (1) *the package,* your résumé; (2) *the sample,* your interviews; and (3) *the purchase*—you're hired!

In hiring, the customer (your future employer) is going to follow the same pattern you did when you bought the soap to clean your blue jeans: the résumé (the package and the label), the interview (sampling the product), and the offer (buying the product). Meet your customer's needs and you will quickly be hired!

THE RÉSUMÉ

14

The purpose of a résumé is not to get you a job but to get you an interview, during which you may be offered a job. Without an effective résumé it is difficult, if not impossible, to get someone to say "You're hired!" It's your passport, your all-purpose tool, the packaging that sets you apart from other candidates on the shelf, vying for the job. The job of the résumé, like the label on the soap, is designed not to include you in, but rather to help ensure that you are not (to paraphrase Sam Goldwyn) "included out."

The résumé is like that tired joke: You can't live with it and you can't live without it. While some use well-prepared cover letters in lieu of résumés, unless your brother-in-law is doing the hiring, we suggest that you don't leave home without it.

Think of your job search as if you were an automobile mechanic assigned to fix a faulty car that's temporarily out of order. Your goal is to fix the car so that it's once again road-worthy and humming along, working hard for you and your loved ones. To fix your career you need specialized tools. The one you'll use most is the all-purpose wrench called the résumé and its trusty socket, the cover letter. Your résumé is the banner by which you are recognized as a prime candidate for the job, the key that opens the door to the interview, the paperwork your future employer needs to start a file on you and justify your hiring to others. It's your sales brochure, your ad campaign, and your calling card, all rolled into two or three sheets of paper, folded into an envelope and sent off to its target.

Although it may take five minutes for you to read your own résumé, it will be scanned by the recipient for a maximum of thirty seconds. In that time it must speak of your professionalism (it must look good), state your goals, and show why you are qualified for their job.

Your résumé is an extension and expansion of your calling card. It lists your accomplishments and points with pride to everything important you have to offer to a new employer, sometimes even your hobbies. The fact that you enjoy cooking and playing the piano is of little consequence unless you are applying to a food or music company, but putting it in your résumé under <u>hobbies</u> reinforces the picture of you as a real person that some unseen bureaucrat needs as justification and encouragement to call you in for an interview. Getting a job is a formalized ritual, and the résumé is its text.

Your résumé must stand out without seeming to. Good jobs have many applicants—as many as several hundred people can apply for one job, all hopefully sending their résumés, which arrive pretty much at the same time on the harried personnel manager's desk. The first winnowing of the pile (and there will be more résumés in tomorrow's mail) is ruthless. Into the circular file go all the unprofessional-looking, badly printed résumés on cheap or oddly colored and folded papers. Next the reader scans the *objective* statement, your summation of the kind of job you seek. If it doesn't match the job on offer—into the trash it goes! If your submission is printed on a good-quality paper and appears to be competent, and if the objective statement matches the advertised job, you may make it to the next phase: a closer reading. Unless your background is so outstanding and the story that your résumé tells is so compelling that it inevitably dictates the choice of you for the job, it will probably be read several more times until it is finally discarded or you receive the good news: They want to see you.

A résumé is about packaging. Remember looking for soap in our little story? Soap is packaged a certain way, so you instantly know, even from a distance, what's inside the box. You could put soap in a soda bottle and the soap would be as good, but why take the chance? Your résumé should look like a familiar product, but stand out in the details. The first step in the customer approach to hiring is to package yourself not to be included in, but rather not to be included out.

Yes, you think you already know what the customer's needs and expectations are, but how well do you really know them? From their ad, from its job description? What are the hidden items? What aspect of the fit isn't advertised, but is critical to the selection process? You, or maybe even the customer, don't really know the exact product specifications until a final hiring decision is made. Then you know that, whatever they are, you fit. Until then, it's anyone's guess.

First point in writing a résumé: Make it as inclusive as possible—work to avoid exclusion.

Excuses, Excuses

What makes the résumé something most of us have such a hard time with? We find it onerous to write and almost as difficult to keep current. Yet, without a résumé, even being interviewed by a friend for a job created just for you is a challenge.

We hesitate in preparing our résumé because we see it as work—and it is. We look at résumés and think: It will be easy to prepare ours. But when we realize that we have to put our entire professional life into two pages, we cringe. A form of writer's block immobilizes us. It is then we realize that a good résumé is the result of real effort on our part, and often help from personal or professional associates.

Most of us have a hard time blowing our own horn. We are reluctant to say what we have done. Bragging is, after all, socially obnoxious—the sign of a bore. Most people view modesty and humility as evidence of good character. That gives us another reason why we don't want to prepare our résumé. Maybe we don't see it as important to others. Shucks, we're just doing our job, after all. What's the big deal? Worse than that is the feeling that if what we say we did was so damned good, why were we fired, anyhow? Another excuse for delay is that we don't know what we want to say. What's the point of the résumé? Don't we need a goal, an objective? Let's wait with the résumé until we get that settled.

Don't do that! You need a résumé and you need it now! Get to it!

Should You Use a Résumé Service?

The résumé is such an important part of the search process that companies exist that will write a professional-looking résumé for you from information you supply. The cost varies but can run anywhere from fifty to five hundred dollars. Depending on where you are on the corporate ladder, you may want to consider this if you can afford to, if the job you seek is worth the investment, and if you don't think you'll be able to write a good résumé without help, or if you are a "résumé-ophobe." Most people don't want to be thought of as blowhards and find writing their own résumés almost as difficult as composing one's own epitaph.

Unless you feel confident about it, you might want to seek help. The résumé precedes you like a paper fanfare. If it is tuneless and toneless and unprofessional you may never hear from the résumé's recipients and never know why. Don't take such risks. If your former company has an outplacement service and you haven't used its cash value to increase your severance, it can help you with your résumé. It's worth using a service as a last resort if for no other reason than to get a professionally organized and professional-appearing document. (It's always better to do it your way and learn from the experience. But do it, one way or the other!)

By scanning your résumé, a prospective employer decides to go further and ask you in for an interview or forget about you and try someone else. The mission of most personnel managers is not to hire you but to find reasons to turn you down if they think you are wrong for the job. Your résumé provides the opportunity to find that reason. Personnel managers keep their jobs not by hiring the right people but by not making mistakes and hiring the wrong people, so they tend to come down on the side of conservatism, in favor of the company and not you. They're not capable of divining from your résumé that you are someone they should take a chance on. Thus your résumé must hit the bull's-eye or they go on to the next one.

Creating your résumé doesn't have to be expensive. There are many books on the market and on library shelves that lead you, step by step, through the process. If you feel confident about this, get a good résumé preparation book from the library or buy computer résumé software and do it yourself. It's the least expensive option and often the best.

Computer résumé programs are all similar, but the big software companies tend to have more sophisticated layouts and typography in their résumé templates. An investment in résumé software saves money in the long run and gives the added option of printing only the résumés you need for each application. It also permits you to personalize each résumé for the company you are sending it to by adding a line to the top, such as "Prepared for the Acme Company" or "Prepared for Jennie Smith, Personnel Director, The Acme Company" and today's date. You can further fine-tune your résumé for various jobs by eliminating the things that are not likely to impress them and emphasizing those things in your career that will.

Be careful not to overdo this. You don't want to create a "gee whiz" reaction that makes them feel that you're too slick for them (or for your own good). Generally you should stay away from colored papers and colored inks and don't use cartoons or other computer graphics on this business document unless you are absolutely convinced that it is appropriate and in good taste. If in doubt, get a professional opinion. Use a good-quality, laid finish, rag bond, white paper* to print on rather than the usual cheap computer paper. You need to put your best foot forward and every detail, such as paper quality, helps the overall impression of professionalism you seek to convey. Your résumé should stand out from the rest, but in a subtle, understated way. Put a sheet of the cheap, sulfite bond typical of most computer print paper next to a sheet of 25% rag, laid finish, bond paper from a quality paper company and the difference will be readily apparent.

The same applies to the matching envelope to put the résumé in. For an impressive presentation, send the résumé unfolded in a nine- by twelve-inch envelope with a short cover letter clipped to it (and don't forget the extra ten cents postage for an odd-sized envelope). An unfolded résumé is an extra touch but underscores that you want to make a good impression. It also stands out from the number ten envelopes everyone else uses and dominates the pile of mail on the recipient's desk. Even

---

*Colored or tinted papers may not reproduce well on a photocopier. Use white stock to avoid such problems.

if no conscious notice is taken of your pains by the recipient, she will be subconsciously impressed and you'll be off to a good start. Keep everything simple and businesslike. Unless you are including samples of your work (for example, to apply for a job writing press releases), stay away from fancy presentation folders and showboating tricks like fancy computer typefaces.

Do your Research

Breaking résumé preparation into steps is a way of tackling the big problem of the résumé. The first step is research. Gather all the details of your work history. First the dates, titles, promotions, commendations, notes—everything that has a bearing on your work history. Now is not the time to be concerned about form; just get the facts down. As you gather them, think about them. Review what you did, when you did it, how you did it, the high points. Think about the details that you'll want to fill in around the facts.

The résumé is your package. It has to look enough like a standard résumé to be sure that you are not excluded (and just a bit better, for insurance). Imagine flipping through a stack of résumés. How much exposure time does each résumé have? Your package, your résumé, the sum and substance on paper of your ability to meet the customer's need, had better make its point as quickly and as strongly as a television commercial, in thirty seconds.

Résumé and Cover Letter Standards

It is creativity within a standardized format that sets résumés apart from each other. Following the standards set out below will not, by themselves, make a great résumé, but ignoring them will increase the chances for exclusion from the final cut.

Cover Letter

Always use a cover letter. It's like the caption on a painting. It tells the reader why you should be hired and your résumé provides the background and proof of what you say in the letter. Many résumé writers are not masters of prose and many potential employers cannot tell from a résumé whether or not they should hire you. The cover letter fills this gap by providing a short sales pitch that complements and reinforces the résumé. They are indispensable and should be considered inseparable. Distinguish the cover letter from the résumé. Use it to make specific points. While you should maintain a consistent model letter containing the points you want to make, to be certain that they appear in each letter you send out, never write the model so that it reads like a form letter. Brevity is important. It should never be more than one page, unless you know a lot more about the job opening than you usually would. Always phrase the cover letter in terms of what you offer, how you can help the hiring person, how selecting you for interview will make the hiring process easier[†]. End the cover letter with a request for a meeting.

A good cover letter is a vital part of your résumé package. If you use a computer and are mailing many résumés, set up a mail-merge file so that each cover letter is individually addressed and the salutation is personalized. Consider sending your résumé and cover letter by e-mail. This involves only the expense of a local phone call and has the dual advantages of getting there instantly, ahead of the competition, and showing off your computer prowess at the same time. Companies are always (and especially now, in these early stages of computer communication) impressed with people who know how to take advantage of the latest technology. If you use this method (or if you fax your résumé—already old-fashioned—everybody does it), be sure to put a backup copy in the mail and reference that fact in both communications. If you are answering a blind ad with only a box number to identify it, your choice of address and salutation are limited. But if you know the name of the company, call the main number and explain that you are applying for the job advertised and want to get the correct name and title of the person your résumé will go to (occasionally it's listed in the ad). Sometimes this information is not given out, but often it's only a phone call away.

[†]Get a bit fanatical about the details of the name and address of the person and company you are applying to. If the person has a title, use it. If he or she uses a middle initial, or has a professional title like "doctor," use it. Get the *exact* name of the company. Getting someone's correct name and address is a sign of respect and care. The same applies to the name of the company. Review the cover letter and résumé with extra care and have it proofread by others before you send it out. There should be no typographical errors, misspellings, or incorrect grammar. Avoid slang or clichés. Your résumé and cover letter are not works of art, but they should look as though they are.

You will make a good first impression, and your letter and résumé will stand out from all the others addressed "To Whom It May Concern" or "Dear Sir or Madam."

Research the Company

Do your homework before you send the résumé. If it's a big organization, there might be stories about the company in the newspaper or industrial trade papers. Check it out in the local chamber of commerce or the business section of your local library. If the company has a public relations department, get its brochures and, if possible, a copy of the annual report and read the president's message to the stockholders inside it [††]. The more you find out about the company's history, its goals, and any other information, the better you can slant your letter to respond to the company's needs as you come to understand them. When you write your cover letter, use this information to show that you are familiar with the company, its products or services, and its goals.

For example, "In the last annual report of the Jones Company, President Jones stated that in the next twelve months his goal is to increase the sales of widgets by 20%." Point out that this is what you did in your last job (if it is true), and you would like to use your abilities to help the Jones Company achieve this goal. Mention the feature story you read about the company in the trade magazine *Widget News,* and congratulate the firm on opening its first office abroad. The fact that you took the trouble to research the company in this kind of depth will be impressive and will ensure that your résumé is read with interest. Be brief with this information and don't overdo it. Is this a lot of work for one résumé? You bet it is. But if going the extra mile gets you the job, would it be worth it to you? Many of your competitors can't be bothered to go to such lengths, so you already have an advantage.

[††] *Insider's Tip:* Find out if the company has a site on the Internet by calling and asking. If the operator doesn't know (many employees haven't gotten the word yet), get the public relations department or the information officer on the phone and ask. Then check out the Internet site. Most companies of any importance now have Internet sites and more are coming on every day. (It's the latest corporate status symbol.) You'll find all sorts of valuable information about the company on its Web site and, if you can work some of it into your cover letter, you'll score points by demonstrating your technical prowess and intelligence, and you'll flatter the company by referring to its Internet site in the letter.

Don't put negative information in the cover letter, either about the company or yourself. The reader is not interested in how long you have been out of work, how badly you need the job, or why you were fired from your last job. (If he is, he will ask you during the interview.) After the first paragraph, which makes a statement that will get attention, the second paragraph should tell what you can contribute to the progress of the company and why. A sentence or two about your skills and abilities to support your proposed efforts for them is appropriate. Conclude the cover letter with a sentence that implies further action, so the recipient knows that you'll be calling or writing again. "I'll phone you next Wednesday, Ms. Abernathy, to answer any questions you may have about my résumé." Be sure you call her on the day you promised to. Many people just send résumés out and sit back and wait. By calling, you get another chance to communicate with prospective employers, to perhaps subtly raise a point in your favor, and to get them used to you a bit. They will see your call as an expression of your sincere interest in their job and also think of you as an aggressive person—just what they're looking for!

Your interviewer will not be the only one to see your résumé. It will be photocopied and sent to all executives in the company whose approval is required for new hires. It will also become part of your employment record if you are hired, so if you customize your résumé for each job, be sure that you have an exact copy for future reference.

Format

There are many résumé formats. One book on résumés lists more than one hundred. Avoid the avant-garde graphic look, unless you know that your customer is looking for that and unless you're a designer with the skill to do it right. The résumé consists of several parts. At the top of the first page, centered, put your name, address, phone numbers, and any other contact numbers such as your fax number. (Don't put your pager or car phone number in.) And if you have an e-mail address, list it.

Summary Paragraph

Use the summary (objective) paragraph at the beginning of the résumé to your advantage. Editorialize and focus the reader on what to expect in the résumé. If you're using a computer or word processor, customize the objective to the specific job. State as simply as you can the position you seek or the type of work you want.

Accomplishments Listing

Write about what you did, not who you were. Remember that you are going to fill a need, so show that you know how to do that. You not only filled the job, you excelled in it. Show growth, comparisons, and use numbers to do that. Then comes your education. List any degrees you may have with the dates and college attended. List your majors and, if applicable, any minors that relate to the job. If your grade point average is good, list it also. List any honors such as Dean's List, Phi Beta Kappa, etc.

Chronological Job Listings

From today backward. It's the best way to show growth; any other format implies that you may not have had growth. The history of your jobs (unless you're just entering your professional life) should demonstrate an orderly progression from one position to the next, each with increasing responsibility consonant with your growing experience and knowledge. The farther back you go in your job history, the fewer details are required. Job listings should start with the position you held, the name of the company, the dates you worked there, and your responsibilities. List your significant accomplishments in each job, such as: "under my direction, the department increased its productivity by 25% in each of the three years I worked there, thereby winning for our division the XYZ Management Award." If you or your team were responsible for advancing the company's goals, especially in the areas of profit, be sure to include it, along with the significant figures. State the facts accurately because they may be verified. It's a bad idea to list the salaries you have earned or the salary you expect to earn in a résumé. Save it for negotiations later on, after you have become an active candidate.* *Never put a salary figure in a résumé!*

---

*By the time you are asked what salary you expect, you are probably in the running for the job. This is a question that should be handled with utmost tact and care. A good response might be "What are you considering offering?" It's an old negotiating ploy, when you don't have a ready answer for a question, to punt by asking a question in reply. This buys you a few moments of time to think and may also uncover important information. An even better response would be "I'm sure your package will be

Miscellaneous Information

After your listing of jobs held, list separately any professional organizations or activities and any significant accomplishments in them. Then
list briefly some personal information that will help round out a picture
of you as an individual. If you have any interesting hobbies, consider listing one or two of them. This will give a picture of you as a well-rounded
person of many interests. Be careful to be brief in this and in all sections
of the résumé.

Explaining Embarrassing
Inconsistencies in Your Résumé

If you have not had a job for more than six months you may be asked
why not. This could create an awkward situation. If you have a history of
changing jobs frequently, or if age or other factors lead you to believe
that a chronological résumé may not work well for you, consider rewrit-
ing your résumé as a functional résumé. This is a résumé that groups
your skills together and lists the jobs you worked on that used those skills.
Leave out the dates you were hired and the dates you left each job. You
can still put dates into the résumé, but deemphasize them by burying
them in the prose. Use dates only when you have to. If you are asked
about it, tell the truth. But you may not be asked. Your goal is not to look
like an unemployable person or someone who will not work there long
enough to justify management's investment in training you into the job.
Think this through carefully because if your interviewers are astute, they
will want to know what you did for the last year. The last thing they want
to see is a sheepish grin and a shrug of your shoulders. Your answer should
be concise, businesslike, and believable. There is no shame in admitting
that the downsizing of your industry has made it difficult to find jobs in
your chosen field or that you worked in your Uncle Henry's restaurant
until the industry recovered from its economic shrinkage. Lame answers
to such questions are the raw meat of cartoonists.

satisfactory. When do you expect the new person to start?" This response not only gives
you added stature but also asks for the purchase (the job) and demonstrates a positive,
aggressive attitude on your part. Don't be too quick to accept the first figure offered,
even though it might be higher than you had hoped. Your success with this question
depends on how badly they want you and how good you are as a negotiator. But by
stating what salary you expect before your interviewer mentions a figure, you turn your
cards over and lose negotiating leverage.

Some Hints on Résumé Style

Your résumé is a tool, designed to do a specific job. The sharper and stronger the tool, the more efficiently it will work. Here are some additional hints to make your résumé work for you:

- *Presentation:* The résumé is you, as far as your customer knows at this time. Misspelled words or typos are immediately translated into the thought that you are careless with details or just plain ignorant. It says who you are, and frankly, it's not good enough. Pay attention to details. Have someone else proofread.

- *Editing:* Make your points clearly and write succinctly. Short bursts break through; long sentences put customers to sleep or confuse them. Use a telegraphic writing style. Unless they show strength, keep adjectives and modifiers to a minimum. In your zeal to make a good impression you may have inserted a few adjectives too many. Cut them out until your résumé reads like a concise, brief business document—which it is. No fluff, just facts. If an adjective is used, see if the sentence makes sense without it. If it does, eliminate it. Edit out vague words like "very," "lots," "perhaps," and "therefore." Break up long sentences into shorter ones for greater impact. Two clauses connected by an "and" may work better as separate sentences.

- *Be Brief:* Edit to simplicity—if it's simple, it's clear. Remember that you won't be present to explain what you mean when a prospective employer gets your résumé. What the customer sees has to represent who you are.

- *Be Specific:* Numbers, comparisons, and percentages show what you can do better than adjectives. "I was a very productive salesman" is self-serving boasting, whereas "I increased sales in my division by fifteen percent per year for four years" is a simple statement of an impressive fact.

- *Be Active:* You are active, so use that voice. Passive writing implies a passive personality and passivity in employment and that is exclusion for certain. If you're not clear on the terms "passive" and "active," get a grammar book and brush up.

- *Be Selective:* This is not your autobiography. It is a brief marketing package. Draw the picture of yourself to show the highlights and downplay the warts.

- *Be Honest:* Ethics count. If you're found out, you lose. Anyone who would lie in a résumé is not making a strong case for fulfilling the customer's expectations.

- *When to Stop:* Your résumé should be short enough in length to encourage reading it but long enough to outline your entire career. The average length is two pages. Three or even four, with lots of white space and wide margins, is acceptable, but more than that, except in unusual circumstances, can create problems. Remember the Irish maxim, "Be brief and be gone!"

- *Proofread, Proofread, and Proofread:* Before you send out your résumé, proofread it several times. Then proofread it a few more times. Then wait a day and proofread it again. Look up any words you are unsure of. Run a spell check on your computer word processor. Then give it to a friend to proofread. If a printer sets the type for you, proofread again with particular care. (Outside typesetters can be relied on to make typos.) A misspelled word or a grammatically incorrect sentence on a résumé is akin to showing up for a job interview with dirty fingernails and soup stains on your shirt.

- *Always Follow Up:* "I'm calling to see if you got my résumé and letter, Ms. Abernathy, and if you have any comments or if I can give you further information." Be brief and polite and get off the phone as soon as you logically can. Don't use this occasion to turn on the charm—just be yourself. Follow up again if you don't hear from the company within a reasonable time after this first mailing and call. A second telephone call to the person you sent the résumé to asking if a decision has been made and reemphasizing your interest in working for the company demonstrates active concern. Many firms appreciate persistence, even if they keep you on hold or tell you "He's in a meeting" every time you call. Be polite and deferential, and never demand anything or be overbearing. Even if someone else eventually gets chosen instead of you, your professionalism will stand out and may get you a telephone call from the company in the future. Polite persistence demonstrates your sincere desire to work for them. But don't make a pest of yourself. A sentence at the end of the cover letter should thank the recipient for their time and for considering you for the position in question. A good cover letter reinforces a good résumé.

- *Follow Up Phone Hints:* Whenever you make an important telephone call like this (or any important business call, for that matter), take a few seconds before you call to clear your mind of distractions. Sit up straight, breathe deeply, and don't lean on your hands or put your body in a position of strain. Don't chew gum, smoke, or jiggle your keys while you talk, and don't type into your computer either, (the call's recipient can hear the keys clicking and it takes your concentration off what you're trying to say). If you want to take notes, use a pencil and pad. If you feel nervous or tense, take a five-minute walk around the block before you make the call. Look into the mirror and smile. While you are thus smiling, go ahead and make the call. Odd as it may sound, a smile affects the tone of your voice as it affects your state of mind. Phone calls like these are small but important steps in gradually overcoming objections and in convincing the prospective employer that *you* are the one for the job.

Your disembodied voice on the phone plus your just-received résumé and letter is all they know about you so far. If your telephone voice is relaxed, businesslike, friendly, even happy, you have scored points in your favor. If you come across as strained or difficult to understand, or if you talk too fast or too slow, you lose points. If you are concerned about your telephone personality, talk into a tape recorder and listen to it. Practice your delivery and play the tape to a sympathetic friend for a critique.

How the Decision Is Made

The decision-making process is composed of two parts. The first part matches you and your background and training to the requirements of the job. The second is how well you sell yourself to your future employer. Assume that there are four or five people with exactly the same qualifications as you applying for the job. How is the final decision arrived at when there are no further objective criteria to consider? Which one of the five will get the job? The answer is: the one the interviewer likes best. The moment of truth during which the decision is made to hire someone is almost always an emotional one. (Call it "intuitive" if the word *emotional* bothers you.) You'll get the nod if you have first removed any conceivable objection to your being hired and when, somehow, the employer instinctively feels that you are "right" for the job. If you could eavesdrop on the conversation in which your interviewer explains to her supervisor why she hired you, you would probably hear words like "There were five highly qualified people who made the final cut. In the end I chose [your name here] *because I felt she could do the job best.*" The final decision was made by feelings and emotions, not logic.

By now you may get the feeling that your résumé is a really big deal. It is—but writing it shouldn't be. Don't get the equivalent of stage fright and procrastinate or evade the responsibility by letting a service do it if you are capable of doing it yourself. Sit down now and write a draft, refine it a bit, and look it over tomorrow. Show it to someone you trust to give you an honest, qualified opinion and maybe do another rewrite, based on any suggestions for improvement. Compare it to other résumés. Ask your friends to show you theirs, or get a book on how to write a résumé and study the examples. When your résumé looks good to you, start sending it out. You don't have time to waste on preliminaries. You'll find out soon enough if it works for you.

Before you mail the résumé, take a minute to look it over one more time. If it still strikes you as a bit wordy or pompous, you can be sure that others will notice it, too. This is your last chance to correct it, even if it means typing the résumé all over again. (This is where computers are worth their weight in gold.) You may catch an error now that eluded you all this time. Did you sign the cover letter? If you don't use printed stationery, is your phone number on the letter as well as the résumé? For an impressive flourish, if you have a fax machine send the résumé and cover letter by fax, with a follow-up copy in the mail. Be sure to note this fact in the fax and follow-up copy. This ensures that your résumé will get there fast and will get attention that may not be given to others. It's also a subtle way of making prospective employers handle your résumé twice and keeps your name in front of them.

If they turn you down on the basis of your résumé, call or write to the person you sent the résumé to and ask why. You will probably get a non-committal response, but you just might get some clues that can lead to an improvement in your résumé or other aspects of your job-hunting campaign.*

Beyond the Standards

Let's review:

- Use general job titles.
- Try to highlight, but not answer all the questions. Tease.
- Show personal job growth, even if titles don't change.
- Use creativity within the parameters; cute and colorful doesn't impress.
- Type the address on the envelope, or print very clearly.
- Be consistent. Include only what is relevant to your job objective.
- Have three to five references prepared and readily available.
- Leave white space, plenty of spacing.
- Double-check for readability.
- Couch objectives in terms of what you can offer.

Computerized Résumé Tracking Tips

- Send an original résumé, not a photocopy. Sometimes photocopies don't scan well. Print a separate copy for each recipient.
- Put your name on the first line of the résumé and put nothing else before it.
- Use a laser or inkjet printer, not a dot-matrix printer.

---

* The same holds true if you are rejected for the job after being interviewed. Try calling the person who turned you down and telling her that you are working on your résumé and interviewing techniques and would like to have their reaction and suggestions as to what you might do to improve your prospects for the future.

- Computerized résumés are often put into a computer database when received by using optical character recognition software. This software is designed to recognize letters by their patterns. Keep the pattern simple by using common typefaces—nothing fancy, no script typefaces. The best typefaces are the common ones: Times, Courier, Helvetica. Don't use shadings, brackets, or compressed typefaces. Avoid being tricky.
- Keep point sizes between 10 and 14.
- Use boldface for headings only, never for name, address, or telephone number.
- Don't use vertical lines, and few horizontal lines.
- Don't use double columns or complicated layouts.
- Use only white paper, 8 1/2 by 11 inches.
- Mail your résumé unstapled and preferably not folded, so it can be properly scanned. Many companies don't accept faxes (so check before you send one), although some do, if the document faxed is going directly into computer storage.
- Use vocabulary and language suitable for the audience.
- Be sure that there are no spelling, grammatical, or typographical errors.
- Neatness counts.

Do Not

This is a long list, for good reason. Any one of these items can exclude you. It's that simple: One reason is all it takes and you're out of luck.

- Do not state salaries.
- Do not include reasons for leaving a previous job.
- Do not volunteer photographs (asking for them is not allowed).
- Do not include personal references on your résumé.
- Do not include letters of reference with your résumé.
- Do not mention references on your résumé.
- Do not volunteer hobbies, activities, or memberships that are not business related.

- Do not include personal information ("married with children") and nothing on religious or political issues.
- Do not send your résumé unsolicited.
- Do not use a cover letter *instead of* a résumé.
- Do not type the word *résumé* on the résumé (recipients know what they are getting).
- Do not include any negative information.
- Do not include a statement of health.
- Do not use nicknames or pet names—maintain professionalism.
- Do not use colloquialisms, slang, buzz words, or jargon not used in the targeted industry.

NETWORKING

15

Executive recruiters can get you a job. A newspaper "help wanted" advertisement can result in a job. Your local state employment office can find you a job. But according to many job experts, by far the most productive and powerful source of jobs is networking. Employment analyst Kathleen A. Riehle, in her excellent book, *What Smart People Do When Losing Their Jobs,*[2] claims that nearly two thirds of all jobs are obtained by personal contact—in other words, networking. While only ten to fourteen percent of jobs come from newspaper ads* and the balance from other sources, you should not overlook any opportunity to find a job. However, your chances of finding a job are probably better with networking than any other source.

---

*Some sources claim that only five percent of jobs come from advertisements in newspapers. The newspapers' figures are, understandably, higher.

Networking is labor intensive, requiring amassing, classifying, working, and reworking long lists of names and addresses and a lot of running around visiting contacts. But you're out of work anyhow, and this will give you plenty to do, with the result that you may find a job.

Networking has traditionally been so hard to define, and even harder to do, that only recently has it become an acceptable term describing a proven method of getting a job. The maddening part is that unless you're a natural-born schmoozer and are willing to really keep at it, networking is hard work. It's hard to define because it involves that old human function: conversation. It also requires constant alertness to possibilities. When Charles W. had completed three months of diligent networking, he finally got a job because he overheard a conversation in an elevator in which someone bemoaned the fact that the head of the data processing department had just announced that he was moving to Canada. Charles introduced himself, identified himself as a data processing expert and asked for an interview, which ultimately resulted in the offer. The whole process resists organization, is not predictable, and is partly based on gossip and guess and partly on luck. However, it's the type of luck you make for yourself by churning your network until it finally happens.

When you urge a friend to see a movie or read a book you liked, when someone tells you to try the new Chinese restaurant that just opened, when you ask a friend to recommend a dentist or stockbroker, when your travel agent suggests a specific hotel—that's networking. The same principles apply to getting a job. When someone recommends you to someone else because you made a good impression, that's networking.

Networking depends on the essential element of all social intercourse: trust. The person you talk to *assumes* that what you tell him is true. He puts his reputation at risk if he recommends you to others because they in turn trust his judgment. If you misrepresent your experience, skills, and accomplishments, you act as a spoiler, not only for yourself but for everyone else who seeks to use this tool. Say whatever you want to your

Accurate statistics on how many people get jobs from ads in the paper are impossible to gather, so it's anyone's guess. What is undeniable is that good jobs are advertised and obtained from such ads, so you cannot afford to overlook this important source of employment opportunities, regardless of the percentages.

contacts, but never exaggerate, misrepresent, or tell a lie.[†] You can be certain that it will eventually be uncovered, to your regret and that of the person who trusted you.

The three basic parts of the network process are:

1. *Creating the network:* It's a living thing, almost. A good network is in constant flux: people move away, die, or come into the area. Once the network is up and running it must be constantly pruned and expanded.

2. *Working the network:* calling your network contacts, making appointments, visiting contacts with specific goals in mind.

3. *Following up:* Just as a waiter does a check-back to see if everything is satisfactory with your order, you must check back with network contacts, keep your job search in their minds, and make sure that the system is throwing off leads for you all the time.

It is precisely because of the informal nature, the human contact side, of this process that it's difficult for many people to perceive it as a process that, if worked diligently and faithfully, in the end will produce results. By applying yourself to this process you continually expose yourself to the market, keep your name in people's minds, and are active. You will also, *if you ask and listen,* learn about industry trends, facts—and gossip. By following up on the gossip, you discover whether it is true and can work for you. In each contact you make you should come out with two or three more names you can contact. That way your network stays healthy, and you keep the game alive until you reach your goal.

The people you ultimately seek in your network sweeps are the insiders, who work in the very places you want to work and who know that a job is going to open up, sometimes before it's announced. They know

---

[†]Okay, I lied! There are times when you can, shall we say, "glorify the truth" if larger goals are at stake. If a man (or woman) wears a wig or dyes his hair to conceal his age, isn't that a form of socially acceptable lying? People habitually misrepresent their ages for purposes of vanity, and there are dozens of stories of boys who lied about their age to get into the army and then went on to distinguish themselves on the battlefield. So when something as important as your livelihood is at stake, is it okay to fudge your age to get the job? If you do so and are hired and turn out to be a wonderful employee, do you really think they will fire you if they eventually find out? You must answer that question but you should ask yourself: "Who will be harmed by this white lie I am about to tell, and who will benefit?"

before word gets out, for example, that the company just landed a juicy contract and needs to hire new staff, that the agency has a new account, that a new division chief is about to take over and plans to increase staff. They are privy to news you need to beat everyone to the punch by finding out about a job beforehand and landing it before someone else does.

However, you don't have an insider list with all the hot contacts. That's the purpose of the network process. But you may have a friend who works in the company, your hairdresser or barber may cut the hair of a division chief in the company, or your Aunt Helen may play bridge with a friend whose daughter knows someone who dates a guy who works there. Networking means that literally anybody you meet in your daily life may be connected to someone who knows someone who knows someone . . . until you finally find the contact you seek and home in with your résumé, cover letter, and follow-up phone call.

If you have a rotary card file or an address book, you have the beginning of your network. It starts with a list of friends, relatives, business contacts, doctors, lawyers, and anyone else whose name and address has found its way into your book. When insurance companies hire trainees to sell their product, the trainees are often told to start by trying to sell insurance to their relatives, then their friends. Each relative or friend is then asked to provide a list of several more contacts who might need insurance. Gradually the network widens until eventually the fledgling agent is selling insurance to people she never heard of, who are introduced to her by others she barely knows.

Think of networking as a large maze. Some turns lead to a dead end. But one of them, followed to its end, can lead to your next job. At each turn sits another person, and there are hundreds, indeed thousands of such intersections, all interconnected. The first ones are people you know: friends, relatives, school chums, co-workers at your former company, even your barber or manicurist. As you probe deeper in the maze, your immediate circle slowly gives way to strangers. But someone you know in the maze has met them or knows someone who has. In the farthest reaches sits someone with the key to your future. Your task is to fire up the network and get it humming, making contact after contact until you finally zero in and find the one person out there who hires you. Once you get the maze into motion, all sorts of things happen you hadn't planned on. People meet you and like you and introduce you to, say, Charlie, over at Paramount Computers, who doesn't have anything for you, but someone you chance to meet in Paramount's lobby puts you on track to your target. Luck sometimes plays a role. But you must put in the groundwork and do all the laborious, time-consuming work to get to the point where your break happens. It will happen if you work the network, if you're in the right place at the right time.

If you buy a résumé software program, consider also buying a contact management program, or one of the newer ones that combine both tasks, by far the most efficient way of keeping track. These nifty computer software packages allow you to list your contacts by name, company, address, and phone number, plus the date you last spoke with them and notes about who they are and why they are important.* Some of them provide basic word processing so you can write letters within the program. There are new programs coming into the stores all the time. *PFS: Resume & Job Search Pro,* †for example, sells for around $40 and creates your résumé, writes cover letters with a built-in word processor, tracks job leads and appointments, and even has a multimedia simulated job interview so you can practice your approach to a new job. There is a career advice counselor in the program and a way to fax résumés and cover letters. Another program, *WinWay Resume 4.0,* also at around $40, suggests ready-to-use words and phrases for résumés and cover letters and comes with hundreds of samples and built-in fonts. It has a contact manager and offers full-motion video (in the CD-ROM version) of simulated interviews and salary negotiation sessions. Most versions of these programs have Internet connections as well. *Act 2.0* by Symantec sells for around $189. It allows you to create your own database of over 70 customizable fields and unlimited data records. It tracks appointments and audibly beeps reminders of upcoming appointments and has a word processor and report generator. These are a few of the many software programs available. These powerful tools that didn't even exist only a few years ago offer professional assistance that gives your efforts the polish and form to impress company executives. They take much of the drudgery out of job hunting and allow you to concentrate on more important tasks, such as working the phone and going out on appointments.

---

*As you put together your network list, note in each record who introduced you to this person and who this person said they would introduce you to in turn. This is crucial to keeping your network healthy and growing.

---

†I am not recommending any specific program. This and the following are mentioned merely to give examples of what's available.

As you search for your customer and assemble lists of contacts, you are putting together a valuable resource that will become priceless if you are ever again out looking for another job—and you will be, according to statistical trends. Employment experts tell us that the average worker in today's work force will change jobs eight times in his or her career. Once you get your job, keep your contact list up to date. When someone gives you a business card, enter it immediately into your contact manager software or, if you don't use a computer, into your contact book or file. Do this at least once a week, more often if cards accumulate. Put in personal information about the contact, anything to help you remember who they are and why you kept the address, and any other information that might be useful, including personal data that you might work into a future conversation. Asking your contact how her new Buick is running or if her back is still bothering her shows your interest and attention to detail and guarantees that you'll make a good impression.

Start scheduling informal meetings with the people on your contact list. Telephone meetings are good and sometimes all you need. Face-to-face meetings are best. Your objective in this string of contacts is to get the word out to as many people as you can that you are looking for a job and what kind of job you seek and to enlist them in spreading the word and putting the links together that will lead you to the company or person where you will find your job. Don't expect the network to go on automatic pilot. It requires you to actively manage it, day by day. If someone promises to get in touch with someone else, call the following week to see if he did. If not, ask politely if it would be okay if you called that person directly, using your contact's name as a reference. Be diplomatic—these people are doing you a favor, so don't presume anything. Most people are happy, even anxious, to help.

As you develop your network list, you'll begin to notice strategic groups.

- *The cool casual contact:* This is a neutral contact who can help start the chain of hot contacts to your job. In this category are relatives and friends, doctors, dentists, and all the people who will act as a flux. They will probably not know of a specific job availability, but they're valuable because they may be able to introduce you to the people who actually work in the areas of your interest.

- *The lukewarm compass pointer:* This is a mid-level contact who is either in the industry you're interested in or knows someone who is. This individual usually knows about the industry, who's who, and often who is looking to hire someone.

- *The hot target:* This contact can be your job offerer or will know if a job is available and who you should be seeing. The target can often introduce you to that person or give you permission to call directly and use her name.

Face-to-face contact is valuable, although not strictly necessary, for the casual contact. The compass pointer and the target contacts should always be activated by a personal visit, unless distance or other factors make this difficult. (They may be in an out-of-state office.) It's important to visit each contact in his or her office, at least for the first visit, and as often as possible in follow-up visits. Why is this? After all, making a telephone call is faster and cheaper.

What you are trying to do in this process of galvanizing your network of contacts is to get into a subjective relationship with them, rather than a cold and impersonal objective relationship. You want to get them to like you and take an interest in you to the point where they will offer some help, sometimes just a clue, about a job or someone who can bring you a step closer to the job you seek. The first reaction of most people is to try to get rid of you. After all, they have more important things to do than to help some friend of their wife's beautician. Think of it from the contact's point of view.*

You may sound fine on the phone, but contacts will probably be reluctant to send you to see someone they value unless they know what you look like first and have had an opportunity to take their measure of you as a person. Their names and reputations, after all, go along with you to the next contact.[†] You not only need to show them what you look like and that you will not embarrass them by your appearance if they introduce you to their contact, but you also need to establish a personal relationship with them, to the extent you can in such a brief visit. "Yes,

---

*In preparing for your contacts, and in almost any other human interaction where you want something from another party, it's a good rule to put yourself in their position and think of your problems from their point of view. Why should they grant your wish? What can you do for them? Is there any risk to them, or any benefit to them, for helping you out? Understanding the other side's view of your request allows you to construct a convincing pitch that will effectively get across your point and bring the results you seek.

[†]Never use a contact's name unless you have his or her permission in advance.

J.B., I met her and I was impressed. She seems competent, makes a good appearance, and has a fine personality." That's the sort of thing you want your contact to say, not "She's a friend of my wife's beautician, J.B. I never met her, but she has a nice voice on the phone."

Each personal meeting with a contact provides an opportunity to get to know you a little better, to like you a bit more, to get interested in your well-being, and to want to help, if they can. It's easier to remember someone you met than someone you only spoke to on the phone because their memory will be impressed with the image of you—or some distinguishing characteristic of yours.

Don't get your contact's guard up by saying anything implying that you will ask for a job. If the contact likes you and knows of a job opening, it will be entirely up to him to mention it. Don't expect it, and make it clear that you are not asking him for "a job." You want his help, recommendations, and advice—and that's all! Everybody likes to give advice.

Presentation: If networking is new to you, you may feel awkward as you sit in your first contact's office, and he looks expectantly at you. You have already figured out your goals for this meeting, but what do you actually say? He will expect you to (quickly) fill him in on who you are, professionally. Tell him your background and education, with mention of any degrees and majors and honors or accomplishments. Then segue into your work history—in two sentences or so (think: thumbnail sketch). You have had so many years of experience and worked for so-and-so, where you were responsible for such-and-such. If you can't write this all down on a three- by five-inch card, you're taking too much time. What he needs is a verbal snapshot of you and your career. At this point your contact is, presumably, sympathetic and wants to help, but you must provide the succinct information that helps make an accurate assessment of you before he can confidently recommend you to anyone else.

If your contact interrupts with a question, ask if you can answer that as soon as you finish telling him about your background. Assume that your meeting will last twenty minutes (one-hour, or longer, meetings are not uncommon); your introductory pitch should be long enough to give your contact a rounded picture of you but short enough not to eat into time you need for developing the contact and accomplishing your goals. Look for body language at around the twenty-minute mark: indications that your contact is getting restless (he loses eye contact with you or glances at his watch). Then say your good-byes and leave. If your contact seems to be deeply involved and interested in hearing more and telling more, prepare to stay on as long as he wants to talk, but mention that you don't want to take up too much of his time. Let him control that for you.

Be Aggressive—Passively: Your contact may be wary, especially if he doesn't know you. Will you embarrass him by asking flat out for a job? Will you waste his time? Do you know what you're talking about? Get around this initial aloofness by being yourself: frank, modest, open about your goals, and interested in his ideas. Suggest a meeting at his convenience, not yours. Use the editorial "we" when possible: "I'd like to call on you next month, Mr. Contact. When do you think we can get together?" "Have we heard back from Mr. So-and-so, the fellow over at Acme Corporation you mentioned in our last meeting?"

Learn: Before you go to see a contact, find out what he does and what his level of expertise is. Try to relate that to your situation, and find areas of commonality. There should be some logical thread that rationalizes your visit.

Listen: You're not there to deliver a seminar on yourself and your industry. Allow your contact time to talk, time to warm to his subject and perhaps become enthusiastic. Ask intelligent questions about the business he is in. Be polite and modest about yourself. Many contacts will sell themselves on you, if only you give them a chance to get a word in.

Share: Your contact has something to gain from you, however limited you may think your experience is. If he has been around for any length of time, he realizes that it's people, contacts, who open doors to the top. You may have news of developments, new faces in the industry, perhaps a bit of gossip. Offer it all. Let your contact get something from meeting you.

Make your visit short and sweet. You have several goals in these contact meetings. In addition to getting the contact to know you on a personal basis, you want to show that you are informed about your business and the industry it operates in, without getting boring or off the track. You also want to be alert for information you can use. Your ostensible purpose in asking for the meeting is that you are making a change and were told by (referrer's name) that Mr. Contact is well informed and might give you some good information that can help as you seek your next job.

Once you state your case and have the sense that things are going well, ask for the sale. The sale, in this case, is more contacts you can call on. If Mr. Contact has mentioned some people in the meeting, ask if he will refer you to them. Your compass pointer contact should know three or four people in the field who can be called on your behalf. If things are going really well, he may even pick up the phone without being prompted and call them. Ask if he knows people you should meet and would he consider calling them so you can make contact. Many people are happy to help, if they can. If you sense some reluctance, don't push. Instead, ask if he would mind if you called them directly and used his name. Most people believe that they are wise and know a lot of people, and here you are—a nice person, sharp, bright, and knowledgeable—asking for their help. You should leave with either your contact making a few calls as you sit there, or giving you names for follow up. You will doubtless find most of these meetings going well because uncooperative people won't grant an interview in the first place. If, however, you find yourself in the office of Mr. Grouch, be polite and leave at the earliest opportunity with a smile on your face. And send him a thank-you note, anyway.

After each meeting on your network rounds, send the contact a short note expressing appreciation. (This is a snap on a computer.) In this age of rudeness, people appreciate someone who embodies old-fashioned thoughtfulness and gratitude. A postcard will suffice, but a short note in an envelope is best, and shows class. Mention something he said that you found particularly valuable. Keep your contacts informed, even if you don't need them anymore. Keep them thinking about you and your job search—you may well need them in future. And networks work in both directions. If you hear of anyone in your network who loses a job, call her up and do what you can to help.

Don't overlook any contact, no matter how humble. Your object is to get the whole world to know that you are looking for a job. As you make the rounds, you'll soon realize that you are not only making many useful contacts, but increasing your knowledge of your industry exponentially and at the same time becoming known to many people. The more you operate your network, the more important your contacts will become, until that happy day when you walk into the right office at the right time. The more you work your network, the sooner it will get you to the person or company you seek. It is the fisherman who goes to the lake every day and puts in the most lines who catches the most fish. There's another hidden bonus in all this networking. When you eventually get your job, you will have established a small army of friends and acquaintances in your field, all of whom (you hope) look on you with favor. They can be of immense use to you (and vice versa) as you go about settling into your job and begin interacting with your industry.

Don't overlook the obvious, either. Your stockbroker, your dentist, your doctor, even the manager of the health club where you work out know a lot of people in various companies. Tell them all about your job search and get back to them from time to time to remind them that you're still looking. When you finally land your job, be sure to tell them about it and thank them for their help, especially if their suggestions led to your goal.

Practice your contacting techniques by doing them. Your first few meetings will be difficult because you won't be familiar with the questions and answers that will soon become second nature to you. As you go along, your techniques will improve. You drop approaches that don't work and innovate new ones to replace them. It becomes easier and easier the longer you stay with it. These contact sessions pay off in other ways. After you get your next job, you'll discover that it's easier to meet people, to call them up cold and arrange meetings that lead to important results for you. Your "people" skills will have developed, along with your presentation skills, your ability to think on your feet, and your confidence that you can go anywhere and meet (almost) anyone you want to. You will also have constructed your private network of contacts—people you otherwise would never have met. You will have some new friends and a lot of confidence that comes with knowing that you can go out into the world and make it respond for you.

ALTERNATE SOURCES FOR JOB HUNTERS

16

"Help Wanted" Ads

Responding to "help wanted" newspaper ads is a way to get a job, but it's not for the faint-hearted. The truth is that you will, in the majority of cases, either never hear from them or you will get a rejection letter, often merely a preprinted form. What an insult! If you're a masochist, you'll just love the daily trip to the mailbox. So why bother?

Classified newspaper ads account for about 5 percent of the jobs secured by clients of Drake Beam Morin, a leader in career-management counseling, according to the company's chairman and president, William J. Morin and James C. Cabrera.[3] That doesn't seem like much, but as these co-authors of the book *Parting Company* wittily note, "these ads make

5 percent of those clients 100 percent employed." The sheer volume of "help wanted" classified ads in most newspapers would seem to indicate that a lot of people are finding jobs in the ads. Newspaper advertising is a catch-all for every type of job imaginable, from waiters to CEOs of corporations and everything in between.

Many job seekers are reluctant to apply for jobs advertised in newspapers because the number of résumés sent that actually result in interviews is so small. While no accurate figures are available, it's fair to state that the probable reason seems to be the very strength of newspaper advertising: its ability to put an advertisement in the hands of hundreds of thousands, even millions of readers every day. Like buying a lottery ticket—along with the rest of the world, your résumé is one of many.

The first few times you pick up the classified section, read it from beginning to end. Organizing this section is at best a random process, and many classifications represent the best call of the editor laying out the section at the newspaper office. For example, a computer company is looking for a salesperson. You might find the job listed in the sales section or under computers—or in one or two other places you might not expect them to appear. Does a job advertised for a salesman of computer services for the medical profession go in the medical help, computer, or sales department? Reading the ads from front to back also exposes you to how a wide variety of jobs are advertised and educates you on how to read them. . .by simply reading them.

As you go through the ads, mark the ones to follow up with a yellow highlighter. This will help prevent you from getting bogged down and confused. Be sure that the back of the same page doesn't overlay your highlighted ad with another one. If it does, photocopy the other side. Afterward, cut out the ads and paste them on a sheet of paper, with the date and name of the newspaper, before you begin the follow-up. Organize the sheets into a notebook or file, and you have the system in place.

While the odds of getting hired from ads are admittedly small, the fact remains that every one of those advertisements is for a job that actually exists and that someone will soon be hired for—someone who took the time to answer the ad. (A few are fake ads, put there for various reasons—read on for details.) If you get a rejection, it will probably be sent by a lower level employee whose job it is to sort through the bags of mail dumped on her desk and pick out the outstanding (in her opinion) responses that merit the attention of her boss. To turn this to advantage you must be a combination detective, clairvoyant, and ace copy writer.

If you're suspicious of personnel departments or have a feeling your résumé might get lost there, consider an end run around personnel by calling the company, getting the name of the boss or the head of the department you are applying for, and direct it to that person. Don't refer to the ad if you do this—the person opening the mail may automatically route it back to personnel—but write as if you are sending the résumé because you just want to work for the company. You can cover your tracks by sending another résumé to personnel, with your standard cover letter. If you are right for the job they will think you are persistent and won't take no for an answer.

Consider going one or two levels higher with your response. If that person walks down the hall with your résumé in hand and suggests to the hiring executive that this is an interesting résumé for the job, you can be certain of a call for an interview. Many executives who will do the actual hiring don't have a high opinion of their own personnel departments, regarding them as a bureaucratic obstacle. If the job, in general, is what you want, but you think that you may be either over- or underqualified, apply anyhow. You can never tell from an ad what's really going on in the company. Bait your hook and drop it in the water. You have nothing to lose and a job to gain.

Read and reread the ad, sifting and gleaning meanings from the few words there as if they were tea leaves, as you try to pierce the typographical veil and decode what they really want and offer. Then fashion a response that mirrors these needs boldly, clearly, and concisely—in the first sentence. In your cover letter, start out with a sentence that implies that you, better than anyone else, can fill the job. The ad may not completely or even accurately represent the job or the company. Copy writers often sugar-coat ads to make them more attractive, or they write them so the company appears larger and more important than it really is, or they exaggerate the benefits and working conditions. Accept what the ad says at face value, but don't believe it completely until you verify it in person.

Your cover letter can follow up with more punchy information that reinforces your first statement and leads to your résumé, attached. Work on the cover letter, over and over, until you have distilled it to its essence, eliminating every word, every adjective that isn't absolutely necessary. Remember, you have thirty seconds or so to grab the attention of the reader and make her think that your letter merits further consideration. If the company's name appears in the ad, do some research on the company if you can. If it's a large company you may find information in the library, or it may have an Internet page. Or try the local chamber of commerce. Any information you get will help you fashion a response that will be provocative, informative, and attention-getting. Most of your competition can't be bothered to go to any lengths, or they don't know how. That gives you an immense tactical advantage and raises the odds of getting a favorable reply.

Daunting as it may seem, you cannot afford to omit any step that could conceivably result in a job, so start your day off with the morning paper (or papers). Consider it your gamble in the job lottery. After all, *someone* will get that job. . .perhaps it will be you. The higher you go on the corporate ladder, the more likely that ads for your job will not appear in the section with two or three lines per ad, but will be in the select section of the classifieds reserved for boxed ads. In some newspapers those ads are not in the classified section at all, but in the business section. If you work in a specialized industry, there is probably a trade newspaper or magazine devoted to it that contains classified advertisements of its own. And don't overlook special papers, such as the *Wall Street Journal* and other financial papers that carry classified sections. If your job has an overseas aspect, or if you seek overseas employment, check out the international press. Magazines like *The Economist* have dozens of "help wanted" ads, many from exotic countries and for unusual and high-level jobs.

Be cautious when answering blind ads (ads that do not reveal the name of the company). Be especially careful if you are still employed—it might be your own company running an ad to replace you or others, or trying to find out which of its employees will "bite" and thus reveal their unhappiness and desire to leave (with the company's secrets), or for a variety of other reasons, none in your favor. Ask yourself what would happen if your answer to a blind ad were shown to your present employer. Some companies run blind ads just to get a file of new résumés in preparation for a planned wave of firings (in which your job may be involved), while others run them because they can't be bothered sending rejection letters. I suspect that at least a few blind ads are run by companies afraid to "disgruntle" someone with a rejection letter; we live in fearful times. Some employment agencies run blind ads to refresh their files of available applicants. Others, admittedly a fraction of a percent, run blind ads and send the résumés out scattershot, to see if anyone responds. The better ones will call first and get your permission (and patronage), but there's no guarantee. Answering blind ads is like shooting arrows into the air. One of them may come back and land on you! If none of the above bothers you, then by all means answer blind ads—just don't expect miracles from them.

Once you have your résumé in order and have settled on a standard cover letter, it's easy to crank out several letters and résumés every few days and send them off. You have everything to gain and not much to lose, except a little time and postage. The secret of answering newspaper ads is simple. Send off your résumé and then forget about it. . .forever. If you get an answer, it will probably be of the "Thank you, but. . ." variety. However, you never can be certain. Perhaps you'll be in that 5 percent who get their jobs through newspaper ads.* To make the ads work for you, it's necessary to send out large numbers of résumés. It follows that you may expect large numbers of nonresponses or letters of rejection. It is important that you not see these as a rejection of your résumé. It's almost always for other reasons, having little or nothing to do with you or your résumé.

Don't overlook work fairs. These are like miniature conventions. Usually located in a downtown hall, convention center, or college campus, they are filled with booths rented by companies that are actively seeking to hire. Call your local chamber of commerce, college or university, or city or state department of human resources for dates and venues near you. Dress appropriately to meet representatives of businesses and bring résumés and business cards. If you're out of work and still have your old cards, cross out the business phone and write yours in (they'll understand), or better yet, go to the nearest storefront print shop (or your computer) and have some inexpensive cards printed with just your name, address, and telephone number on them.

Warning: You can't afford to overlook the classified ads or any other source of jobs. However, if you are spending an inordinate amount of time on them (remember, only a small proportion of jobs come from this source), it may be a signal that something is amiss in your job search. Some people are naturally shy and don't enjoy going into unknown environments or speaking to strangers. Sudden reliance on the job ads may come after many rejections for jobs and might signal job-search burnout. If you can honestly (and courageously) admit to yourself that your concentration on the classified ads is a form of escape or procrastination, you have made an important insight. If this is the case, go to an employment counselor or a psychologist and root it out of your mind.

Headhunters

If you are called by an executive search firm, or headhunter, take it as a compliment. A company is willing to pay a search firm the equivalent of one-third of your first year's earnings to get you to work for them. You're not required to pay the headhunter for finding you a job, and it will quite probably be the job you seek. These firms are several levels above employment agencies and handle managers and other executives, all the way up to CEOs. Whether you go to an employment agency or an executive search firm depends on what kind of job you want. Generally speaking, staff jobs, such as designers, accountants or bookkeepers, researchers or writers, should register with an employment agency, preferably one that specializes in the field. Managers or executives are probably candidates for the executive recruiter. Even if you aren't in that category, don't overlook them entirely. Sometimes they take a lower- level job search to accommodate a client or friend or simply because they like you and want to help. The largest handle applicants whose compensation is in six figures, while the smaller, one-person firms (and there are plenty of them) accept clients with lower expectations.

The best of them operate on high ethical levels. They seek companies as regular clients and, once anointed by their client, are given all the executive searches from that company. Companies usually use one executive recruitment firm at a time, and recruiters take care not to poach each other's territory. The very best of them tend to be exclusive. Their reputation, and repeat business, depends on the caliber of candidate they offer. This makes them difficult to crack for many job seekers. The best way to get registered with them is be referred by someone they know. However, job seekers come to them unsolicited as well.

Résumés are their stock in trade. They need a constant supply. Get your résumé to as many of them as you can with a short, businesslike cover letter. You can get their addresses from the trade association that serves your industry or profession (the business section of your library will have the American directory of associations—and don't overlook the foreign ones), the telephone directory, the human resources department of your ex-employer, the Internet, and recommendations by friends and business acquaintances. After you have your next job, it pays to stay in touch. You may expect to change jobs often in today's business environment or even (Heaven forbid!) be fired again.

Many of them do not interview candidates initially. They simply categorize and file your résumé. If you have a résumé on file with such a firm, send them a new one every six months or so. Older résumés are usually discarded after a time because they are assumed to be out of date and also to keep down the volume of résumés that must be filed. When a search comes in, current résumés are reviewed and the likeliest prospects selected. Then they call and conduct a telephone interview. If you survive that, you're usually called in for a personal interview where your qualifications for the position are discussed. One of the largest, Korn Ferry, only operates through the mail. You send them your résumé and wait. If a position opens that fits your qualifications, you'll hear from them.

The Disposable Job

You may be lucky and get another job in a few weeks. But don't plan on it. Most people who have been fired take two to seven months, sometimes more, to connect with a good job. During this period your first priority is to campaign for your next job. But you may be short of cash if you haven't put any aside. You also may be nervous and worried.

A way to take your mind off your problems and keep some cash coming in while you wait for the big opportunity is to take a disposable job— a job that's easy to get, with minimum qualifications, flexible hours, and not too much physical or mental strain. You need a willingness to work at a humbler occupation than you were in, with the knowledge that it isn't a permanent career change, and enough flexibility to jettison false pride. Disposable jobs should be considered when your unemployment benefits run out. This is not only because you will no longer qualify for benefits when you take such a job, but also because while you're on benefits you have 100 percent of your time to devote to your real task—finding a job. A disposable job cuts into your time and energy, so consider it carefully.

Ken S. was fired as regional director of sales for a company that publishes yellow pages phone directories. He had a two-year apartment lease with another year to go on it and had just broken up with his fiancé. Ken was a thousand miles away from his Ohio roots, lonely and crushed by the turn of fate. His dreams had turned to ashes, and he didn't know what to do. So he did nothing. He sat in the back patio of his apartment and worked on his tan, sipping cold sodas and listening to the radio, vaguely hoping something would happen. His life was on hold; he was mentally paralyzed and couldn't break the spell of his self-imposed isolation.

His landlord, an avuncular man with two sons the same age as Ken, took pity and had a fatherly chat, advising him to take any job, just to get out of the house and back into the world. Ken was waiting for something like this, although he couldn't articulate it or define his problem if asked. He jumped at the suggestion.

He walked three blocks to the diner where he ate breakfast and asked the manager for a job. He was hired as a waiter and began working the same day. For the next eight months he worked six days a week and filled in evenings for other waiters who needed time off. Ken is nice looking, with a charming manner and a gift of gab. His salary was modest, but he did well with tips. Soon he was walking around with a roll of bills in his pocket.

He quickly made friends with co-workers and liked to invite them to the apartment on weekends for a card game and barbecue. He had broken the spell and found a new life. He forgot the lost love of his life when he started dating Kathy, one of the waitresses. A few months later he struck up a conversation with a customer who owned an advertising agency. He was offered a job as a junior account executive and took it. That weekend Ken had a barbecue on the patio, and he and Kathy announced their engagement.

Other "disposable" jobs are taxi driver, security guard, and retail clerk. If you apply, don't show your résumé or tell them that you're only applying until you get a job in your regular line of work. You might find yourself refused on the grounds that you're overqualified. The less they know about your intellectual and other accomplishments, academic background, or career track the better your chances. What they all seek is an honest, hard-working employee with a good disposition and no major problems (drugs, alcohol, a history of crime).

Disposable jobs are easy to get and easy to quit. They leave no mark on your résumé and have the advantage of keeping you out in the world, engaged, and working your network. They also provide some hard-earned money and most of them won't wring you out emotionally, although some can be physically trying. Perhaps their greatest advantage is that they reinforce your character by proving that you can rely on yourself no matter what happens, and that you are not too proud to take any job that will move you forward.

Volunteerism

If money is not a problem, consider volunteerism. Hundreds of organizations, large and small, are looking for volunteer workers. These include church groups, civic organizations, fraternal societies, political parties and special-interest political groups, environmental organizations, public radio and television, hospitals, museums, and libraries. Whatever your interests or skills, there's an organization that would love to have you volunteer your services. Nonpaying jobs available run the gamut from envelope stuffers to telephone workers, announcers, museum docents, guides, typists and computer operators, and a full range of executive positions, some of which come with salaries.

There are over one million nonprofit organizations in this country, employing an average of eight people each. Many have staffs (both paid workers and volunteers) numbering into the hundreds. They go under the general names of associations, nonprofits, and foundations, and include schools, social service agencies, hospitals, religious institutions, political groups, government and local community agencies, sports organizations, and cultural institutions (museums, symphonies, dance and drama troupes) in almost any part of our vast and varied culture.

They all need people to come and work, and the rise to the top is sometimes easier in such organizations than in the commercial world. Some of the top (salaried) jobs pay well, although never on a par with industry jobs. However, they often offer great personal satisfaction—the chance to work where your efforts can make a real difference in society.

This is a great way to network with people who can help your job effort. Volunteers in organizations are the doers of the community, people who want to change things for the better. Many are highly educated and have contacts and connections that could prove valuable. Working as a volunteer has an edge of excitement and participation in something important that many jobs lack. It's never boring, and you may get opportunities to do things you never would have a chance at otherwise. In addition to the networking opportunities, there are other compelling reasons to volunteer.

Many organizations that utilize volunteers often hire the best and brightest for paid staff positions. In addition, working in an exciting environment takes your mind off your problems and keeps you in tune with the real world. There are people out there whose problems make your situation insignificant by comparison. Such focus is good for the soul.

Finally, you get the satisfaction of knowing that you make a difference, that your efforts, humble though they be, are helping a good cause. Are we our brother's keepers? the Bible asks. You bet we are!

The Little Job that Wasn't There

There are two kinds of jobs that never get advertised. The first is the job where "they" come to you with a wonderful offer. People in the stratosphere of business like former superagent Mike Ovitz and the man who hired him, Disney chief Michael Eisner, are typical of this rare breed. Others in lesser but still stratospheric corporate slots are regularly wooed by executive recruiters. This category includes (but is not limited to) academic professors in various disciplines, lawyers, advertising executives, top CEOs of large corporations, athletes, coaches, team managers, art directors, copy writers, and other individuals whose skills and talents have made them so desirable that they are besieged with offers.

On the other end of the corporate scale is the job that doesn't yet exist. "The best kind of job is the one you create yourself," say the pundits. This is a challenge usually available to those whose careers are just getting started and who possess what was once called moxie, but is now known by an earthier term. If you are a plucky sort, with lots of energy, and are willing to put up with some hardship before your career takes off, perhaps you should consider this route.

Arthur O. moved to a picturesque town in the American heartland and opened a small art gallery with his life's savings. Because the gallery was based more on hope than on logic, he had to close it two years later and take a job as a draftsman in an engineering company to survive. A creative sort, he vented his frustrations occasionally by writing well-crafted letters to the local paper. One day the editor phoned and offered him a weekly column for a small stipend, which he could write without interfering with his bread-and-butter job.

Arthur enjoyed doing the column and decided that writing might become his career. He applied to the state division of tourism for a job as a writer and enclosed his résumé and samples of his column. The director wrote back politely that there were no openings but that his résumé would be kept on file.

Arthur kept calling and writing the director every few weeks, sending his columns as they appeared in print and requesting a meeting. Finally he was granted a short interview during which the director, hoping to forestall Arthur's persistent intrusions, stated as firmly as he could that there were no openings and that the department was fully staffed. Rather than take the hint, Arthur was energized by the interview. He stepped up his campaign, sending newspaper and magazine clips of interesting stories about the state's tourism industry to the director. After several invitations from Arthur, the director finally agreed to have lunch with him. Arthur selected a restaurant and on the appointed day showed up with his wife, an attractive and charming woman.

After three months of this relentless campaign, the director caved in and hired him (probably just to get rid of him, Arthur speculated gleefully at the time). However, once ensconced in his new position as an information writer, he discovered that his immediate supervisor, an experienced newspaperman, had a drinking problem. Sensing an impending problem, the director had apparently hired Arthur to train for the supervisor's job.

Sure enough, eight months later the man disappeared for three weeks on a monumental bender and, upon returning to the office, was fired. Arthur was promoted and given the title of chief of information of the department. This was the beginning of a career as a tourism writer and travel industry executive. Once he got past the initial resistance, the director began to appreciate Arthur's positive virtues of persistence and dedication and his writing skill. As the director put it to me, "I adopted Arthur." When the opportunity arose to hire someone, Arthur was the obvious choice. This is the kind of job that never gets into the newspapers, that no one even knows exists until it has already been filled. It was a job created by Arthur, although it came to him through the hands of others. Had Arthur not made a pest of himself (in a nice, polite way), the director would undoubtedly have put up with the increasingly frequent absences of the problem employee for a much longer time.

The advertising industry has many executives who began their careers as interns, working, sometimes at no salary to start, as a "gopher," doing odd jobs and toiling in the agency mailroom, then moving up the ladder. Many of the top executives in the advertising world credit their start to such humble beginnings. They are valued because by the time they get to the top they have worked in every department and thoroughly understand how an advertising agency works.

If you would like a career in (fill in the blank) but no one will hire you because you have no experience, you may want to consider working for free, or taking a job as an intern, if you can find one. (Some companies are increasingly reluctant to take on free-of-salary trainees because of recent litigation and IRS decisions that they pay taxes; the fact that the employer hired the individual and didn't pay a salary does not relieve the employer from his tax obligation.)

Keep your job-hunting antenna going all the time. Get into the habit of reading the financial section of the newspaper, as well as the rest of the paper and many magazines. Drop into your library once a week and read other magazines and newspapers. What you're looking for is news of a new person taking over a company, a new company being formed, important developments in your field that could lead to the creation of new jobs. This is a vast area which requires putting two and two together and concluding that these developments may signal new jobs. If you're diligent, you may find yourself showing up at a new company before the paint dries on the walls and long before any jobs are advertised through the usual channels. You'll certainly get their attention, and perhaps admiration for your enterprising attitude. You might well be just the kind of go-getter they're looking for, and you'll have the field all to yourself because the others are either too lazy to do the research or not bright enough to think about it. It could be a lot of fun and an excellent adventure!

THE CHANGING WORLD OF EMPLOYMENT

17

Are You a Knowledge Worker?

The term *knowledge worker* sounds modern with a touch of the arcane. It has the linguistic ring of "miracle worker," a sort of shaman who can infuse knowledge into a lump of clay. Fantasy aside, there are over one million of them in America today and their ranks are increasing at the rate of 25 to 30 percent each year. There will be more than two million of them by the year 2000 and they will grow exponentially into the foreseeable future. Furthermore, they are well paid, entering the work force right out of college with salaries in the $30,000 to $40,000 range and going up to $150,000 and beyond for the top jobs for an experienced person.

Who are they, these enviable workers? They're the vanguard of the information age, the work force of tomorrow. They are people who deal with knowledge, and, as such, they will control many of the levers of power in the information age worlds of business and culture. They are architects, computer programmers, teachers, marketing experts, computer engineers, television and film technicians, researchers, and Internet-related technicians, among many others. The list goes on and on—some professions newly hatched to meet the needs of today, others as old as civilization itself. What they all have in common is that they work with knowledge and not brawn. As standard industry jobs in manufacturing, construction, oil, and steel are increasingly automated and computerized or sent overseas, premium jobs of tomorrow will go to people trained to use their brains in specialized ways.

Can you qualify as an information worker? You'll need at minimum a bachelor's degree in business, engineering, or liberal arts. A master's degree is even better. According to the U.S. Department of Labor, jobs requiring master's degrees will be among the fastest growing, around 28 percent by the year 2005.[4] High-paying jobs will grow faster than low-paying jobs, so the key to job security in the world of today and tomorrow is education.

"And Now ... in Glorious Technicollar!"

It's a new world! The delivery man punches a hand-held computer before he hands you your package, and you "sign" the receipt with a stylus on a rubber pad that translates your scrawl into pixels. The office secretary has been replaced by an assistant who doesn't do shorthand but is a whiz at WordPerfect and Lotus, while her boss, in the next room, is busily typing his letters into his PC and e-mailing them around the world or across the room! No wonder today's job market is so often daunting.

Please welcome . . . the worker of tomorrow! Many of the once-traditional blue-collar and white-collar jobs have been morphed into what Secretary of Labor Robert Reich dubs the technicollar worker.[5] Only a step or two below the knowledge worker, they are paid a solid middle-class salary and are in the fastest growing job sectors. The bad news is that technicollar workers require more education than the average blue-collar worker (but not as much as the knowledge worker). Minimum is a high school diploma and perhaps a year or two of college or other specialized training.

More good news for technicollar job applicants: There's a critical shortage of them that's not likely to be met for a very long time. According to surveys conducted by the National Federation of Independent Businesses,[5] the shortages are threatening the growth of business and slowing the nation's economic progress. It's usually up to the individual to get this training because companies are reluctant to spend money training workers who can then leave for a better job, taking their expensive skills and training with them. This empowers technicollar workers by making them less dependent on the company for job security and more dependent on the quality of their training and experience, thereby neutralizing to some degree the threat of being fired. Once established as a bulwark of the new age-of-information economy, the knowledge worker and the technicollar worker will become the core of a new and more secure middle-class prosperity.

Who are these new workers? Is there a place in their ranks for you? According to Secretary Reich, they are hospital technicians who run tests and perform tasks once handled by doctors; paralegals who research cases by computer and prepare computer documents for attorneys; graphics technicians who work for architects, engineers, and designers; financial technicians who run specialized software for accountants, auditors, and brokerages; sales clerks who now use hand-held computers that simultaneously print the receipt, schedule delivery, and replace the sold item in inventory; secretaries who plot spreadsheets and access the Internet; repairmen who use hand-held computers to diagnose problems; coal miners who operate computers to send robots into the mines—even the automobile repairman who fixes your car with the help of one computer and analyzes your smog levels with another—and dozens of other jobs in a bewildering assortment of trades and industries.

Figure out what you like to do, and, if you can, get your degree in that, if you don't have it yet. Then take an entry-level job in that field. It's probably a good way to ensure that you won't get fired again.

GET YOUR JOB ON THE INTERNET (AND A LOT MORE, TOO!)

18

If you're not using a computer you're hobbling your career. If you are computer literate but not yet on the Internet, get on it right away, if you can. A computer turns your table top into a versatile powerhouse to help you get another job. It's invaluable to many job seekers and will soon become indispensable. Not only will it get you onto the Internet, with all the wonderful resources for job hunting, but it will write your résumé and cover letter, keep track of your contact network, address mass mailings, print the envelopes, and let you play a few games while you wait for the phone to ring. It will even dial the phone for you and keep track of the call so you can use the expense as a deduction from your income tax, which it will also calculate for you.

According to Michael Wolff, who publishes an online career resource guide called NetJobs, "Because of the Net's efficiency in terms of how it brings together employees and employers, within a few years there will be no other way to get a job except by this medium." Wolff claims that there are over 1,000 Internet sites devoted to this subject, with more being added all the time. While Wolff may be forgiven a bit of hyperbole, an important part of the Internet has been devoted to careers, job opportunities, and related subjects. According to Kathy Sims, director of the University of California at Los Angeles's Career Center, most colleges and universities have a Web site that lists job opportunities.[1]

The advantages of job hunting on the Internet are undeniable. You can do it in the privacy and anonymity of your home, for one. Imagine looking for a job in your pajamas! You can do it twenty-four hours a day, maybe even find a job lead during one of those sleepless nights while you worry about getting fired, or hired. Jobs are listed in your city, state, in other states, and around the world. Greg Thomas found a job with Oracle Systems Corp. in San Francisco while cruising the Internet on a laptop in his parents' home in New Jersey. He used other net resources to change his career path from freelance writer into a legal assistant in Oracle's software division.[2] Most services on the Internet are free unless you want to use some of the supplier's services that cost money, such as personal career counseling. You can send thousands of résumés to companies over the Internet at no cost to you except a local phone call and what you pay to your net provider each month. Best of all, it's fun!

Jumping into the Net can be daunting and time-consuming if you have no plan—there's a bewildering variety of resources there, with more added all the time. Unless you already know where you want to go with your career, you might start with a skills assessment service that gives you a profile of your skills.* Then use a service that matches your skills to various types of jobs and professions. When you have inventoried your skills and decided what type of job you want, you can use the Net to research various companies that need your abilities. You can approach these companies cold by first reading about them at their Net sites and then sending your résumé and cover letter, if appropriate. Finally, you can start winnowing the thousands of job listings on the net, using the criteria you established. Once you have your job, find out from the Net how you

---

A good outplacement service not on the Web will also conduct a skill and personality assessment for you.

can get child-care help or what the options are for opening your own business, if that's where you think your future lies. Check out the chat rooms provided by your Internet carrier. You'll be able to exchange information about job hunting, get advice, commiserate with others in the same boat, find the latest industry buzz, gossip, and maybe get some real leads. There's almost no limit to what's available. With the Net and a computer, you're in business!

A list of all the job resources and related services on the Internet demands a book of its own. [†]In addition to the sites listed here, surf the Internet to find more. When you're on a site, you'll notice some underlined words, usually in a contrasting color. These are links. Put your cursor on one and if it turns into a little hand icon with a pointing finger, click the icon and it takes you to another linked site. When you're finished, you can easily click back to where you started. Additional sites are coming online all the time. Here are some worth checking out:

1. **Your Personal Network**
   (http://www.ypn.com)
   Michael Wolff's NetJobs site contains an online version of his career resource guide and Resume-O-Matic, a free fill-in-the-blanks résumé builder. Start by clicking on **jobs** in the left-hand column and go from there.

2. **The Riley Guide**
   (http://www.careermag.com/newsarts/jobsearch/1036.html)
   A clearinghouse for career information.

3. **The University of Waterloo**
   (http://www.adm.uwaterloo.ca/infocecs/CRC/manual-home.html)
   Use this site to assess your professional working skills.

4. **Smart Business Supersite**
   (http://www.smartbiz.com)
   Get free career advice on this award-winning site. Among the many features it offers are access to association directories,

---

[†]*Pam Dixon's and Sylvia Tiersten's 398-page* Be Your Own Headhunter Online *(New York: Random House, ///1995; $16.00), is a comprehensive book about job hunting online. It takes the reader step by step through finding jobs online, creating and posting an online résumé, and creating your own home Web page.*

résumé distributing links, a message board, and mailing lists. It's a good resource tool for all sorts of applications to the business of finding a job.

5. **Occupational Outlook Handbook**
   (http://www.espan.com/docs/oohand.html)

   Your tax dollars at work! The Department of Labor lists over 250 occupations, comprising eighty-five percent of the jobs in the country, enumerating educational requirements, job conditions, and earnings potential.

6. **AT&T 800 Directory on the Internet**
   (http://att.net/dir800)

   Search by name or category for the company you want to work for. If it's listed, you'll find its toll-free number here. This site is lightning fast, but a brief tour of its capabilities is desirable to make maximum use of its sophistication and power.

7. **Directory of Executive Recruiters**
   (http://www.careermag.com/careermag/)

   Career magazine's Web site for finding executive recruiters in all locations. For a fee, you can post your résumé here for six months, where it, presumably, will be seen by executive recruiters.

8. **Department of Health & Human Services Administration for Children, Youth & Families**
   (http://www.acf.dhhs.gov.)

   The Child Care Bureau of this government department can be of help as you seek options for child care, a vital career component for the single mother or two-career family. Start by clicking on "ACF Programs and Administrative Services." At the next screen click on "programs," and go from there. There's loads of good information here, especially for low-income families, minorities, and those with special needs.

9. **New Ways to Work**
   (http://www.nww.org)

   Loaded with up-to-date information about alternative work arrangements, telecommuting, job sharing, flextime, and part-time work.

10. **Employee Benefits Research Institute**
    (http://www.ebri.org)

    Check out the benefit packages available to industry and compare them with what your prospective employer may offer.

11. **Women's Bureau, U.S. Department of Labor,**
    Work & Family Clearinghouse
    (http://www.dol.gov/dol/wb/welcome.html)

    Presents the facts about the status of women in the U.S. work force. This site is a "must-visit" for women and should be read by everyone, male or female, employer and employee.

12. **Jobtrak**
    (http://www.jobtrak.com)

    This site is available only to college students and alumni of over 400 universities around the country. You'll need a password to get into it. (Apply at your university's career center.) Once you're into the site you'll find over 200,000 listings of companies that have jobs available and are looking for qualified applicants.

13. **Yahoo's Business Library**
    (http://www.yahoo.com)

    Yahoo (yes, that's its name) maintains this as part of its many offerings. Yahoo is one of the most powerful search engines on the Net, and its Business Library is full of information you can use in your job search. Suggestion: Type "business library" in the dialog box (be sure to enclose words in quote marks) and hit search button.

14. **List of Trade Journals and Associations**
    (http://www.yahoo.com/Business and Economy/Organizations/Professional/)

    Here you can browse through the trade journals appropriate to your chosen field for employment listings and news about your industry. If the URL (above) doesn't get you all the way to the full address, just follow the menus and keep adding words until you get to the list of journals you seek. This site is loaded with useful information.

15. **Electronic Trade Journals**
    (http://www.lib.uwaterloo.ca/discipline/More_resources/journals/subject.html)

This ponderous site can be trying for the impatient seeker. But if you persist and don't mind the plodding software and some irrelevant pages, you will be rewarded with invaluable background knowledge for trades you may be interested in.

16. **Listing of Newspapers Online**
    (http://www.yahoo.com/News/Newspapers/Regional/)

    Keep clicking on the lists provided by each successive page until the top line is structured just the way you want it to be. You will end with a page of names that should be exactly what you are seeking. Then click on the publication(s) you are interested in.

17. **Career Mosaic**
    (http://www.service.com:80/cm/)

    Here you'll find many job listings plus in-depth company profiles. If you want to work for XYZ Corp., look it up here. If it's listed, you'll get a company history, goals, and structure. Many list a contact person to whom you can write or send your résumé.

18. **The Monster Board**
    (http://beast.monster.com:80/)

    Jobba The Hunt, a cartoon character, will help you find your job on this visually appealing site. Post your résumé here, then research companies you're interested in worldwide. Afterward, browse over 50,000 ads for positions open. The site also has specialized job listings for the medical field, CEOs wanted, etc.

19. **Careerpath**
    (http://www.careerpath.com)

    You can access over 90,000 (on an average day) jobs by newspaper name, job category, or keyword. Registration is free and covers seventeen cities (Atlanta, Baltimore, Boston, Chicago, Columbus, Denver, Hartford, Los Angeles, Miami, Milwaukee, Minneapolis/ St. Paul, New York, Orlando, Philadelphia, Sacramento, San Jose, and Washington, D.C.) plus southern Florida with both blue- and white-collar listings.

20. **Jobhunt: On-Line Job Meta-List**
    (http://www.job-hunt.org)

    You name it and it's probably available at this site. If not, there are links to Careerpath and the Monster Board. Learn how to write a résumé, how to hunt for a job, look up employers and recruiting companies, or delve into links to specialized listings in various fields and professions. It's a supermarket of resources.

21. **Disgruntled**

(http://www.disgruntled.com)

Take your mind off your troubles with the online magazine to get re-gruntled. Articles, chat rooms, etc., make fun of and vent anger about various workplace subjects including Roasting Turkeys (horror stories about bosses), Men's and Women's Gripes, Corporate Resolutions (what the boss should do), Inhuman Relations Department (more horror stories), Getting Gruntled (the way back to workplace happiness), and How to Avoid Drowning in the Secretarial Pool. An icon of a scowling boss, when clicked, hides the magazine and substitutes a harmless document.

IT'S INTERVIEW TIME! ARE YOU READY?

19

Preparing for the Interview

You did everything by the book (this book, we hope). You sent out résumés, you worked your network, you surfed the Internet for jobs, you read every tiny-print advertisement in the classifieds until your eyes teared—and answered many of them—you stood in line dutifully at the department of human resources to attest that you tried to get a job last week, and you really did follow up every lead, including the ones your Uncle Harvey gave you that didn't pan out (as you knew they wouldn't). Slowly the days passed. Nothing! Then one day it happened! Your telephone rang and it was *them,* the position you hoped against hope you would get. They want to see you as soon as possible, how's tomorrow? You swallow hard and agree to be there at the appointed time.

Hold it right there! Stop the projector! If you haven't prepared yourself for this most important step, the one that will bring you right into the castle, rewind the tape now and start preparing yourself because the call will always come when you're not ready. You don't have a clean suit. Your car is on the rack, getting a new transmission. You twisted an ankle and have to hobble around with a crutch for another week. Worst of all, you don't have a clue about what to say or do during that crucial interview.

You'll solve your problems. What you need to do first is the same thing you needed to do that day your ex-employer said to you "You're fired!" You need to get control of your emotions and clear your mind for sober thought. If you're a jogger, go out for a run. Or take a long walk. Or call your mate and share the good news. Do whatever it takes to let off steam—but don't do anything that will prevent you from getting a good night's sleep and waking up tomorrow with a clear mind.

You will probably not be hired during the first interview unless the situation is unusual. (For example, perhaps all the interviews have been completed except yours, and perhaps when your interviewer got half-way through your interview, it occurred to her that you are the best candidate for the job, so why not decide now. She may have gone into her supervisor's office for approval and come back having decided on you.) More likely, management has narrowed their choice down to the point where they have either decided on you—but first want to meet you in person—or they have several other finalists and want to decide which to pick. If it's a large company you will be interviewed by a lower level person. If you pass that interview, you'll be called back for a second interview, and this time you will probably receive their offer. You will control that meeting because whether you take the offer or not is up to you. In that delicious moment you'll experience a rush of excitement as you realize that your life is no longer on hold. You are again in charge of your destiny and the healing, while not yet complete, is in the home stretch. The second interview will be by a higher executive, possibly the top one.

The Day Before the Interview

The day before, tend to your appearance. Get a haircut or have your hair done. Have a facial and do your nails, if that's what you normally do for a big event. Fuss with your clothes and decide what you'll wear the next day—nothing too casual, but not too dressy either. If you're unsure, get advice from someone whose taste you trust. Take out the outfit you want to wear and examine it for flaws. In the movie *Patton*, George C. Scott—among many memorable scenes—had one that applies to everyone preparing for an important encounter. He stood before a mirror, putting on his uniform and getting ready to go out and win the Battle of the Bulge in World War II. Like a knight, he slowly and deliberately put on and fastened every button and buckle in his uniform. When he was ready, he went forth to do battle—and to win.

That's the winning attitude you should have after you dress for the interview. When you know you're looking great, you can relax and concentrate on the session. Be absolutely certain that everything is in place and, when you are finished dressing, you look as good as you can and are dressed appropriately, not to win a war, but to take back the career you lost when you were fired—and continue your march toward your future. For that's what will be decided during the interview—your future, at least as far as your next position can bring you into it. This is your final ordeal. Pass it and you're back in the saddle again!

The Big Day

On the morning of the interview, rise early and eat a hearty breakfast. Allow plenty of time to dress leisurely and properly. It's important to enjoy this happy process. You will be building confidence and getting into a positive frame of mind—necessary preliminaries to project the image that validates their good opinion of you so far. A little extra time is also good insurance to be able to fix a broken strap or a missing button you didn't notice before.

Arrive at the appointed place early. Arriving too late, even by five minutes, is unforgivable, so allow enough time. You can always stroll around the neighborhood if you're too early. Depending on the company and the job you're applying for, you might try going inside to wait. It could yield information that might be useful, such as a conversation with someone, or just a look around to get familiar with the environment. The interviewer may make you wait if you get there early, but you have demonstrated promptness. The interviewer may not notice your promptness, but you can be sure that she'll notice if you're late. Little things that are normally unimportant take on larger-than-life symbolism during periods of decision, when judgments have to be made. If you show up late, even with the best of excuses, you will be forgiven politely, but you will have planted a suspicion that you're a careless person who cannot be on time when a job is at stake. You have worked like a hero to get to this point—don't take chances on damaging your credibility now, or after you have the job secured. Be prompt and on time, now and forever!

Manners Create Perceptions

Some people think of manners as a throwback to the quaint past, useless rituals indulged in by dilettantes. The fawning fops in the comedies of Molière and Marivaux are ridiculous figures whose richly exaggerated manners falsely flatter their superiors, a practice worthy of ridicule. But good manners are central to human interaction because, as a form of body and vocal language, they express respect and consideration. No one appreciates the boor who dominates conversations, never listens to what others say, and interrupts in midsentence with pompous, empty bombast. Good manners demonstrate our humanity, our empathy with the feelings and conditions of others, and our awareness of their needs. It is for all these reasons, particularly the last, that you will be judged, if only subconsciously, by your manners during the interview. Whether your interviewer shows up in a three-piece suit or jeans and a T-shirt, he will be sizing you up for how well you fit into his corporate culture. Boors and bullies will quickly be weeded out and manners are the best way of determining that, short of getting to know the person over an extended period of time.

If you had a good night's sleep, ate a hearty breakfast, took a hot shower before dressing, and are happy with your appearance, you should be feeling pretty good about now. Relax and just be yourself. The interviewer will be sizing you up to see if your personality is a good fit with the rest of the staff, how you respond to questions, how you express yourself, what your confidence level is. (That's why the preliminaries are important—you can't afford to be distracted during the interview with concerns about your appearance.) You are, in a sense, wooing them, trying to win them over. This doesn't mean that you have to do a song and dance or recite a speech. Just be your genuine, competent, nice self. Smile easily, and when you speak, do so clearly and loud enough to be heard. If this all sounds elementary, it's surprising how many people get stage fright and freeze up during an interview, mumbling responses to questions with a strained expression on their faces. Your interviewer will assume that you will be a trifle nervous and will be pleased to discover that you act in a relaxed, natural manner. A lot can be forgiven during an interview, but why give the interviewer anything to forgive you for?

Interview Preparation Checklist

- *Rehearse:* If there is time, go through another interview rehearsal using a friend as interviewer, or practice in front of a mirror, playing both roles. The more you rehearse, the more you will relax during the interview and concentrate on substance.

- *Review:* Review all relevant correspondence and notes. Reread the printed information about the company, its annual report, brochures, stories. Go into the interview with this information fresh in your mind. In particular, review the requirements for the job and match them against the experience you have, as outlined in your résumé.

- *Names:* Don't put yourself on a first-name basis unless invited to do so. Call your interviewer "Mr." (or "Mrs." or "Ms.," whichever is appropriate) and get the pronunciation of his last name right, even if you have to ask how it's pronounced. Don't call your interviewer "ma'am," or "sir." Get the interviewer's correct name and use it.

- *Greetings:* When you walk in, greet your interviewer with a big smile, shake hands, and use his or her name in your greeting: "Good morning, Miss Abernathy, I'm pleased to meet you." Shake hands and greet by name anyone else participating in the interview. You are off to a good start.

- *Eye Contact:* Look into the eyes of whomever is talking to you. Give that person all your attention. When you answer a question or say something, look the interviewer straight in the eye. If you look down at the floor, out the window, or up at the ceiling when talking or listening, you lose.

- *Body Language:* Keep your hands in your lap unless using them to make a gesture. Relax your body naturally, but don't slump.

Don't worry about feeling nervous—you're expected to be apprehensive.

- *Responses:* While the interview is not a military ritual, neither is it a gab fest. Answer questions fully, using examples if required, but don't ramble on, tell jokes, or get off the subject. Try to make your answers short and to the point—businesslike. When you feel you have answered the question—stop talking. Your résumé was read by your interviewer. Don't repeat it in the meeting, but if asked, state the information in a different, more conversational manner.

- *Goals:* The purpose is to convince the interviewer that you are fit for the position by virtue of your past experience, training, schooling, and career objectives.

- *The Bottom Line:* If you know your stuff, improving your interviewing techniques will help you get the job. If you don't know your stuff—nothing will help!

Be prepared with information about the company, but don't volunteer it unless the opportunity arises. If your interviewer tells you about the new factory in Indiana, you will score points if you mention that you read about it in the annual report or the *Wall Street Journal* and were impressed with its size, "250,000 square feet, wasn't it?" Sit there with a blank stare and no responses to your interviewer's statements, and you may soon notice a chill in the room.

It's not a good idea to take the initiative unduly, unless given the invitation to express yourself. Confine your responses to answering the interviewer's questions. Make asides or remarks as appropriate, but stick to business. Your interviewer knows what she wants to find out about you. Don't obstruct her plans or distract her by throwing out irrelevant or premature questions.

What the interviewer wants to see is someone who is eager to start work, knowledgeable, and able to help the company meet its goals. Note the word "knowledgeable." The interviewer will not expect you to know all about your new responsibilities, but he will expect you to have a working knowledge of the business and what your job will be. Your responses don't have to be of the "Golly . . . gee whiz!" variety, and you will definitely be out of line if you start grilling the interviewer (or even asking politely) about when to expect your first raise and when you get a vacation. This is the surest way to find yourself quickly back on the street. Save these (legitimate) questions until the company has committed to hiring you. That's the appropriate time to bring them up. Until then, don't ask what they can do for you, to paraphrase President Kennedy. The interviewer's purpose during this session is to find out what you can do for the company. If you offer what the company needs, then you'll be the one who will get the job.

Good luck! Break a leg!

INTERVIEW OVERVIEWS

20

Sampling

Remember, earlier in the book, when we used the packaging of soap as a metaphor for packaging your résumé? Let's continue that line of thought for a bit as we consider how the customer (your future employer) samples the product (you) prior to making a purchase (hiring you).

It's an interview, whether or not you think so, and the first one may be by phone. Every time you make contact with your customer, it counts. This is sampling. It isn't feasible that you do the sampling—you're the product, remember? Throughout the process, which may consist of one or many interviews and may include testing, try to project your actions and reactions in the interview toward how well you will do the job, if hired.

There is no casual conversation—everything you say or do is presumed to be a reflection on how well you'll meet the need, fill the job.

AN IMPORTANT T.I.P.

- *T:* Time is of the essence. Once committed, you must be prepared to drop everything when the customer (employer) calls. This cannot be stressed enough. Timing is *everything*. Schedule all interviews, meetings, and phone calls as soon as possible for two reasons: (1) by acting first and fastest you may just preclude further searching, and (2) what the customer wants, you want. Make it as easy for her as you can.

- *I:* Don't be afraid to think of yourself. Nothing you are doing now is more important than your future. Right now this is bigger than anything, including your current (or former) job. Don't let anything stand in the way of securing the best for yourself.

- *P:* Prepare, prepare, prepare. There is no such thing as too much preparation. The more preparation you do, the more confident you'll feel, the better you'll present yourself, and the more advantages you'll have for a successful campaign.

The Interviews

There may be one or a series of interviews, depending on the needs of the customer to sample their impending hire. We'll talk here about three types of sampling:

- Doorkeeper Interview
- Testing
- Decision-Maker Interview

There may be additional testing. There may also be peer-group meetings and interviews. There may be interviews with outside consultants or recruiters at any time in the process. The interviews may be conducted by phone, video taping or conferencing, or even by e-mail. Remember: All are interviews. No matter how friendly everyone seems to be, it's all part of the sampling process. Everything you say or do is taken as reflective of what you will say or do on the job. There are first impressions, there are last impressions, but there are never no impressions. Every word, every action counts!

Are you ready for the interviews? Stop, and right now, before you go any further:

- Update references information and contact them.
- Get a good-quality version of your résumé (later make three to five copies).

Doorkeeper Interview

Your first interview is often conducted by a person whose job future rests primarily on not making mistakes. Before this person opens the door to the opportunity, you will have to convince him that you should not be excluded, that you should be passed through. You move through the door by making a positive impression and by—and this is crucial—*not being in any way negative.* People get shut out in the doorkeeper interview for the following "nots":

- Not saying or doing the right things.
- Not making a positive impression.
- Not showing enough interest in the job.

Listen, Focus, and Mirror

Listen: The most important part of any interview, especially the first, doorkeeper interview, is to listen. Devote all your attention to what the employer is saying and, if the interview is in person, what his body language is saying.

Focus: The next important part of any interview, especially the first interview, is to focus on what you've heard. Keep your thoughts on what has been said and focus on your answers, which are in turn focused on the specifics of the questions.

Mirror: Mirror what you have heard and focused on back to the interviewer. Tell him what he told you, from your perspective. Don't offer objections. Don't ask what they can do for you—rather, show what you can do for them, in terms of their needs and your background.

Don't be afraid of the interview process. Most interviewers are not terribly skilled. Prepare, of course, as if they were, and that way you are prepared for any eventuality. You and the doorkeeper are equals. As doorkeepers, they want to hold the door open—they don't want you to fail. Your success in getting through the door means less work for them. They want a job to get filled sooner rather than later.

But they don't want to be embarrassed by you at the next interview, either. A typical doorkeeper knows that any credit to be gained by introducing and supporting a good candidate is diminished by each candidate who proves inept, embarrassing, or utterly unsuitable in the follow-up.

The key words for the first interview, whether with a doorkeeper or a decision maker are *Be Positive*—in your actions, qualifications, and interest.

Positive Actions

You have to look positive, mentally and personally. Confidence comes from preparation. It is natural to be a little nervous about an interview. But you'd better not show it. And you'd better be prepared—but you'd better not show that either. Let's review some basic confidence builders:

- Know where you're going.
- Get yourself into a positive frame of mind. Just as the coach gives his team a pep talk, full of cornball sentiments, just before the game (and it works!), you must get yourself into the frame of mind that will turn disadvantages into advantages. Read inspirational literature and advice books. Stay away from the vampire and horror books when you're preparing for an interview. Pump your mind with powerful positive thoughts. Read something funny at breakfast and put a smile on your face when you walk in for the interview.
- Be "The Little Engine That Could." Don't even think of failure. If you don't think you'll get the job, how can you expect your interviewer to?
- Make sure you know when you must be there and who the contact is, plus the phone number if you need to call. Write the information on a piece of paper and keep it with you at all times.

- Call and confirm the appointment. It's appropriate to call for directions or to verify correct spelling of names, etc. Usually it's better to speak with administrative persons when making queries, but don't be embarrassed to ask anyone higher up a question. It's better than being late because you didn't have the correct address and got lost.

- Be prompt. Of course, people have been hired who were late for job interviews. You only hear about those hired, however. No one who was late and wasn't hired because of it will tell you about the incident. They probably still don't know why they weren't hired.

- Dress for success, one level above the level of the job for which you're being considered. In today's workplace casual attire is more common than it once was. But don't be fooled. The casual dress could easily conceal a hard-driving corporate culture. In any event, if you are professionally attired, you have made a positive statement. Anything else is risky. After an initial interview, you may feel comfortable in dressing down or enjoying a casual day. Short of being ridiculous, stay with your professional attire, one level above the job.

- Before you walk out the door, inspect yourself. Do you have a handkerchief? Are your socks matched? Any runs in hosiery? Are your shoes shined? Are all zippers zipped; all buttons buttoned? Sounds obvious, but you'll be in a "hyper" state of mind and you just might overlook something simple that will cause you embarrassment later. Brush your teeth just before leaving and take some breath mints before you enter. If your breath smells from coffee, tobacco, garlic, or onions, you're in trouble. If your breath smells from alcohol, cancel the interview and reschedule.

- Be prepared. Carry, at a minimum, two to six copies of your résumé and a note pad and pen. You never know who might ask for your résumé. "Look, here's Jack, why don't you talk to him? Jack needs to know who you are." Your résumé gives Jack the opportunity to participate in hiring you with some knowledge, and the time it takes him to read it allows you to further prepare yourself for the unexpected.

- Write down the details. You don't need to take notes of the digressions of your interviewer, but what about the time and place of the next interview? What about the correct spelling of names? What about the notes you may want to make after the interview? These are appropriate note-taking opportunities.

- Know the customer. Knowing about the opportunity is a great confidence builder. Read up on the company, research, ask friends. Find out as much as you can about the company and the job. Most of this knowledge is not going to be used, but it's better to know more than you say. Knowing gives confidence, and confidence shows. It shows positive.

- Relax . . . and visit. Visit ahead of time (or arrive early and look around). This will help give you the flavor of the working environment. By being on site early, you tend to get comfortable. Allow enough time to get yourself together before the interview. Relax and go over your preparations. Be cordial but not chatty—you are visiting (and quite possibly being observed).

- Be polite . . . and relax! It goes without saying (or does it?) that you should be comfortably polite to everyone you meet. If you have properly prepared, you should not be nervous. You should be comfortable not casual, confident not nervous, positive and . . . ready.

Positive Qualifications

A Note About Testing

Your résumé preceded you; now it's time to listen for what the real job needs are. But while you listen, don't slide into a passive mode. Speak, but don't dominate the conversation or get off the track. In our sampling analogy earlier in the book, we suggested testing the product before you buy. Because you cannot try out a job before you decide to accept an offer, it's impossible to fully test this product. If anyone is testing, it's the new employer, who tests you in an unspoken (but real) trial period once you are on the job. However, the principle remains operative because you can test the product verbally during the interview process. This is accomplished by asking carefully phrased questions about what the responsibilities will be and what challenges (read: problems) the new employee will face. Ask questions that are designed to get information about the position, and bring up anything in your experience that demonstrates your ability to handle that information and shows you as capable and informed. However, be careful not to overdo this, or to appear to take the momentum (control) away from the interviewer. His decision to make the offer (or not) is the source of his control. Once the offer has been made the power shifts in your favor, so before you actually accept the offer is the time to do your verbal testing. At that time it will be considered proper for you to ask many questions, and they will (usually) be eager to answer them for you.

After the offer has been made (you've convinced the company —now they are waiting for you to accept), and before you have accepted it, is the period of your greatest strength because they will then be sold on you, and you still have the power to refuse. Once you have accepted the offer and been hired, you have surrendered your independence and agreed to be their employee, thereby giving them power over you (now the specter of being fired comes dimly over the horizon as a faint possibility). You will always have the power to quit the job (and if they value you, it's not something they want you to consider), but that is an option not lightly taken. If your testing during the interview takes the form of intelligent probing, it will probably be regarded as the sign of an aggressive employee—something most employers would want. But handle the questions you ask as if they had lit fuses attached to them.

- Listen to hear for what the job entails. Is there anything in your background that specifically fits this need? Have you done something similar before? The doorkeeper is not looking for someone who can do the job, he's looking for someone *who appears to be able to do the job.*

- Be a spin doctor. You can't change your résumé, but you can put a spin on a particular aspect, if you hear a need and have an experience to tell.

- Rehearse your answers in advance. Improve your qualifications by having good, prepared answers for some of the more common questions:

  1. "Tell me about yourself?" Don't start when you were five years old; instead, redirect the question. "Where would you like me to start?" or "Is there some aspect of my background you'd like me to talk about?"

2. "Why do you want this job?" Have an answer, your personal, positive answer, ready. Keep it brief but specific. "It's time for me to grow. I want to join a progressive company. I can learn a lot from your company."

3. "How did you meet challenges?" Have ready some specific examples of successes, and if not successes, how you grew and learned from a challenge.

- Prepare for tough questions: "Why did you move?" "Why did you leave that job?" Think about your background as shown in your résumé and have the answers ready.

- Never say anything in any answer that is negative, in any way, about a previous employer or situation.

Positive Interest

The doorkeeper wants to forward those people who are motivated. Show your interest and motivation:

- Answer every question by showing what you can do for the company and not asking what it will do for you.

A Few "Dos" and "Do Nots" to Keep in Mind

If your operating premise is to stress what you can do for the company if they hire you, rather than what the benefits to you will be, you are sending a wonderful series of positive messages: You are unselfish, you are dedicated, you are cooperative and eager to help, and on and on. If your main thrust is to find out what you can get from them, you will send out messages of disinterest and greed that will work against you. Read this entire section of the book over before you go on the interview and keep the following points in mind as you walk in.

DO NOT

- *Do not* ask about pay. If you are asked, deflect the question with something like "I'm sure you have a strong package. When would you like the new employee to start?"

- *Do not* ask about retirement, benefits, etc. When asked, say what you currently have, but don't apologize or give any indication of dissatisfaction.
- *Do not* be negative about your current or past employers. If you badmouth them, how motivated and mature can you be?
- *Do not* put your interviewer, or anyone else, on the spot. Don't ask "What happened to the person who held this job?" Ask instead, "Why is the position open?" Make it easy for the doorkeeper.

DO

- *Do* maintain a positive attitude.
- *Do* sell yourself.
- *Do* show that you are interested in and want the job.

Begin preparing for your next interview as soon as you leave the first. Before you go to bed on the night you had your first interview, make a written copy of your notes of the interview, being as complete as possible. Write a thank-you note to the interviewer. A short, handwritten note is fine. First paragraph—Thank you for the interview opportunity. Second paragraph—Cite an additional selling point for yourself, referring to something mentioned in the interview. Third paragraph—Express your interest in the job.

Decision-Maker Interview

The point of this interview is to get a job offer, or at minimum move the process forward. This is the time to discuss what you can do for the prospective employer, not what he can do for you. Don't raise objections. Don't ask about irrelevant issues. After you have been selected for the job is the time to consider what the employer is willing to offer to get you.

- Be sure you have learned as much about the employer as you can. Don't act as if you know their business cold, but do have some feeling for what the company does and how it operates. Use your available references, but don't ask friends unless you can be absolutely sure of their maintaining the confidential nature of the inquiry.

- Don't discuss money.

- Be consistent. The question "What have you been doing?" may be asked. Focus on your response. Perhaps you might answer the question in a manner to promote yourself, such as "Would you like to know how I? . . . " Since you have listened for problem areas, you can now focus in on how to solve them. *Note:* Some of the questions asked by different interviewers may be the same as those asked by others in previous interviews with this company. Be consistent in your answers and polite. Don't say "I gave that information to Ms. Abernathy last week." Simply consider the question as if it had never been asked before and repeat your response if it was appropriate. If the interviewer asks "Do you have any questions?" mirror your response with something like "What exactly are you looking for in (candidate position)?" Listen, then match your skills to fit the need. When the interviewer asks "Do you have any other questions?" ask "What is the major problem you'd like me to tackle first?" Then mirror the interviewer's response by explaining how you have solved similar problems; focus on specific illustrations and detail (without exhausting the interviewer).

- Always end an interview with an expression of interest. "Yes, I'm interested in the position, and believe I have the background to do it. Where do we go from here?"

- Send a thank-you letter. Don't wait—send it the same day as the interview.

- Keep all your contacts confidential. You have been presented confidentially, and the employer has been advised to maintain confidentiality; maintaet into the middle of your job-hunting process, and none of them can work to your advantage.

THE JOB IS OFFERED: YOUR MOVE!

21

What Is Negotiation?

The job offer and the negotiations for terms and conditions will usually take place at the same time. That is why when the offer is made you must immediately shift into your negotiating mode. Let's see what negotiation is all about. (Your actual acceptance of the job may also take place during this meeting, or it could occur at the next meeting.)

Forget the mystique. Some people make a big to-do (and a lot of money) writing books and lecturing about it. But born negotiators are just that—people with the personalities and skills needed to get the best deal in a negotiation. They are virtuosos of verbosity who can think on their feet and talk circles around most people. They often gravitate to professions where such skills are desirable, such as the law, commerce, politics . . . and talk radio. The rest of us only occasionally need to negotiate formally.* All it means is coming to an agreement, in this case about the terms of your employment. Your new employers will tell you what they want to pay, what your responsibilities will be, where you will be situated in their offices, how much vacation time you will get, and all the other things you need to know about your new job. You can either accept what they offer or object to whatever doesn't agree with your idea of the job and propose your own idea of what's desirable instead.

Look into your psychological makeup and carefully examine your feelings about negotiation. Many people mistakenly think that any discussion of terms or any attempt to get a better deal is somehow shameful, the thing proper folks don't do. By this interpretation, all those who try to get better terms or a better price—on anything—are a few steps above a peddler. They are the folks W. C. Fields had in mind when he said, "Never give a sucker an even break." Your future employer doesn't think you're a sucker, but if you have some reservations about the terms offered and you don't voice them or argue for your terms, your new employer may wonder about your negotiating skills when you are working for him and if you will be capable of getting the best possible deal for the company you will shortly represent.

The only thing shameful about negotiating during the employment interview in which the actual offer is made is in not doing it, particularly if you're not satisfied with the terms of employment. If your position is reasonable and well thought out, and you present it politely but firmly, it should be met with care and consideration, and the responses should be equally reasonable and well thought out. This is the pressure point at which, psychologically, the wound you sustained to your psyche when you were fired will reopen. You won't be well served if you let it happen.

It's worth reminding yourself that you are being hired, not fired. You are once again on the reality side of the mirror and not on the other side, with Alice in chaotic and clueless Wonderland. Your employers came

---

Almost any interaction between people could be interpreted as some form of negotiation. Deciding what to eat for dinner or what restaurant to go to, buying anything from a pair of shoelaces to a car, planning a vacation—all involve at least some negotiation. Even making love is a bit of pleasurable negotiation. Why many Americans view negotiating with distaste is a puzzle to people all over the globe. Bargaining (a branch of negotiation) is normal in much of the world and for many people part of the enjoyment of shopping. One who accepts the first price quoted is often considered a fool.

into this meeting thinking that you are the best possible person, maybe in the whole world, for this position. They want you to work for them because you have convinced them—with your résumé, your subsequent follow-up, and now your appearance and presentation—that you are the best qualified person for the job. If there is any flexibility and if the person hiring you has any power at all, he will be inclined to grant reasonable requests or demands you make. That doesn't mean that your every wish will come true. But it does mean that your requests will be politely heard and if there is any way of meeting them, he will try to do it. Your interviewer does not want to go to his boss and be told, "You mean you let the most qualified person to apply for this job go over a few piddling dollars?"

Your employers will not reject you because you ask for more. Rather, they will respect you for valuing your skills and abilities highly. Keep in mind that the decision to hire you has already been made. Now it's merely a matter of the details.

We have suggested role-playing in other parts of this book, and other books on the subject also advocate it. This is something you should try well before a job offer comes in. While you're still out of work, trying to find a job, you must pretend that you have one on offer and are negotiating for the best deal. You need a good imagination, but it's worth the effort. Find a trusted friend or relative who can role play the prospective employer and act out the interview not once but several times. Each time, have your partner in acting change the responses so that you don't know exactly what's going to be said.

Before you reject this suggestion, think a bit. By acting out the interview beforehand you'll be able to anticipate what may be asked or what the responses might be and get a chance to develop your positions accordingly. It's another way of thinking about your future. You'll get another substantial benefit from this exercise. By pretending to interview for a job offer you will condition that stubborn subconscious mind of yours to the reality that you are worthy of being hired, that a job is out there just waiting for you, and that when you find it, you'll get it. That's no small thing.

It's not a coincidence that role-playing—shall we say—plays a role in dozens of situations far more meaningful than a job interview. When a presidential candidate (or any other aspirant for high office) is preparing for a hearing, a speech, an interview of importance, he role-plays with his staff, who throws hard questions at him so he's prepared when they are really asked. Astronauts role-play the entire mission, rehearsing over and over (in their case in multi-million-dollar simulators built for the purpose). When police train for their profession, they role-play making arrests and questioning suspects, in realistic settings.

By acting out a situation you are able to formulate positions on various issues and accustom your conscious and subconscious mind and your emotions to hearing words and phrases from others and hearing them from yourself. While the actual event may not resemble your rehearsals, you will be psychologically prepared for almost any eventuality and will have responses stored in your mind, ready to help. It's far better to respond with a clearly thought-out statement than to mumble, "Well, er, I actually hadn't thought of that," or worse, just sit there in confused silence with a blank look.

While you may not be able to predict what will be said, you won't go into the meeting in ignorance. You now have a good idea of the job and what it pays in other companies. If you don't, find out. Seek out people who might know or go to the library or other sources that can provide that information. By the time you get to the interview you should know about similar jobs, what they pay and the kind of experience and education needed, and the story of the company advertising the job—that is, its history and position in the industry. Is it large or small, a start-up or a long-established firm? Did you read its annual report and other material?

If you are prepared, you will have been able to use the first, exploratory interview to ask questions and do some subtle probing that might give you clues to the company's position that you can use to advantage in the final interview. You should have a clear idea of what salary is acceptable for the position and what salary you want. If there is a discrepancy, use the rehearsals to develop arguments to justify a higher salary. These arguments put forward your skill assets and what you bring to the firm—your education, your previous experience, your accomplishments.

Take your time. Your interviewer has no more important job to do today than to get you on board. Be polite but take time to develop your thoughts. The longer it goes on, the better your chances of prevailing. This is largely an instinctive judgment. You should be able to sense when you're going too far. By the same token, don't be afraid to take a few risks as you present your position. Your new employers will either grant your wish, modify it downward until it is acceptable, or reject it outright. If they modify it downward, try to pry it up a bit if you can. If they reject it outright, suggest that you might want to discuss this a bit more. Be alert to body language and tone of voice. Keep pushing for advantages, but realize when the game is ended and stop negotiating. Then you may accept their deal or reject it, or accept with reservations. Perhaps you can get them to shorten the time before you get your first raise if you meet their goals, whatever they may be.

The higher the position for which you are applying, the more there is to negotiate (stock options, bonuses, etc.) and the longer the negotiations will take. In some high-level positions negotiations can drag on for several meetings over an extended period of time. Everything is subject to negotiation.

Be polite, courteous, relaxed, and friendly and respect the time and the nature of your interviewer. That is, if he or she is humorless or curt, accept it and work around it. Your interviewer may be a hack or the most gregarious, friendly, and wonderful fellow you've ever met. You are both actors in a play; play your role and strive for your goal.

One final reminder: When you have both agreed on all the terms and conditions and your interviewer has indicated that the job is yours, and you will start working at the agreed date, that's the time to start planning for the possibility of your getting fired and start planning your next move. Those events are probably a long way off, and, in fact, they may never arrive, but these are difficult times. Forcing yourself to face those realities, as far-fetched as they may seem at this happy time, will bring your mind into focus from the euphoria of being hired and will be healthy for your state of mind in this new job. The life preservers on the deck of every ship are not put there for decorations, despite their attractive appearance in movies and stage sets. Get your job preservers in place as soon as you're safely aboard, before you set sail and become too preoccupied.

The Offer

Get the job while getting the best deal. It seems so obvious, yet so many positions hit the rocks when the offer is finally made. A certain giddiness sets in, the job seeker's equivalent of combat fatigue. You've been out there so long that when a job finally arises, you may become a bit reckless and say things that don't help your cause.

The making of the offer is a negotiating session, even if it's not pre-sented as such—it's not a bargaining session. At this point you and your new employers are "in love" with each other. They really want to hire you, and you really want to work for them. Any doubts have been resolved, and the way is now clear for the final hurdle. These are, to continue the romantic analogy, the "prenuptials," the details of how it's going to hap-pen, how you're going to come aboard so both sides are satisfied that they got a good and fair deal.

Everything is on the table now. There are no further substantial ques-tions remaining. And of all the things on the table, almost anything can be developed in your favor. They will make the offer. You must try to rec-ognize what, in the offer, you can change and what you can't.*

At the core of every offer is salary. You have handled everything masterfully up to here. But it's not over yet. The most dangerous shoals still lie ahead. The company is definitely interested in you; your gut tells you that they want to make an offer. You are getting euphoric and can smell victory. Your position up until now has been "What can I bring to you to make this job and this company work better?" You haven't even mentioned your needs yet.

Don't mention salary or any other benefits, or anything at all about your needs, until they tell you, in no uncertain terms, that the job is yours. The closer you get to that commitment, the more danger there is of los-ing it all at the last moment. If they bring up the subject of salary before the offer is definitely made, counter with a statement like "Your com-pany has a good reputation. I'm confident that the salary you offer will be acceptable." If they persist, ask, politely, "Are you offering me the job?" If they say no, not yet, tell them that you would prefer to discuss com-pensation after they make up their minds that you can do the job and have decided to offer it to you. They have already decided what the job is worth. You may have made such a good impression on them that they may revise it upward. If you mention a salary that's either too low (you don't value yourself enough) or too high (you have an inflated idea of your worth), you have a problem.

---

*Warning: *Beware of performance-based compensation plan offers. If this is on offer, get it in writing, especially for management and executive jobs. Getting it in writing prevents any "You must have misunderstood what I said" situations from developing. When you receive the written offer, remember that it's an offer, not a contract. When you accept the written offer, you have been hired.*

If the offer is too low, you can try to negotiate it higher. You should have a good idea from your research and your network contacts what such a job is worth. When the offer is finally made, you may discover that it's higher than you expected. At that point you may try to get it a bit higher by giving them a good reason. Your reason should be linked to what you can do for them.

Executive recruiter Robert Rintz, managing director of Renard International–USA/Los Angeles, told me of a client who, after going through the entire process, was offered a salary of $48,000. She thought about it for a few moments and then said to her interviewer, "I can't help it. I envision myself at this point in my career with a fifty-thousand-dollar salary." "Done!" said the interviewer. At this juncture, said Rintz, it's like a love affair. Both the employer and the candidate want to consummate the deal and "get married." Neither one wants any obstacle to stand in the way, now that they have both gone through a complex courtship. The employer is anxious to get her started as soon as possible, now that the selection process is just about over. The candidate is equally anxious to get started in her new job, to get back on the salary track, to get out of the purgatory of joblessness. "It is almost always possible to get another five percent higher in salary or the equivalent of that in other benefits," Rintz says.

Remember, other benefits may well compensate for a salary that is not quite what you wanted. You should ask for a salary you think you are worth without being unrealistic. But if the salary is within an acceptable range, take it if you really want the job. Don't lose a good opportunity because you held out for a higher salary than the company wanted to pay. If you're a good choice, you'll become indispensable and your employer will provide adequate compensation later. If the employer had refused the request for another $2,000, the candidate's next move would have been to try to negotiate its equivalent in other benefits, or to tie in the raise with reaching an agreed-upon goal in an agreed-upon period (such as a performance bonus)—that is, a salary increase unrelated to the normal raise she might expect . If you can't raise the drawbridge, try to lower the river. In the end you will take the job, but at that point the employer, having prevailed, owes you one and should be looking for an opportunity to give you the raise as soon as he can justify it. In many positions formerly acceptable salary levels for certain jobs have gone down, while others have gone up in some industries. If your offer feels right, take it and worry later.

The Nuts and Bolts of Negotiation

A good negotiation is, unlike a legal encounter in a courtroom, not an adversarial procedure. One side should not win while the other loses. In a successful negotiation both sides win. Both sides come away with something and can then work together afterward in harmony. By the time you arrive at the negotiation (offer) stage, you will probably have met and been interviewed by several people and will have visited the office one or more times. Ideally, you should already know your negotiating partner and have formed the beginnings of a relationship based on trust. This is not always possible, but it is highly desirable for success in this important last step. If there is any way you can get to know your negotiating partner before the final negotiation takes place, do it. Perhaps a visit to his office to better understand the company, perhaps an impromptu lunch, perhaps a drop-by visit to give him or her a document or some promised information. Negotiations are based on trust and that can only be established over a period of time.

1. *Your Goal in Negotiating:* Go into the negotiation with a clear goal. What salary do you want? What responsibilities do you expect? What about perks such as medical plan, retirement, stock plan? Think it through until you have a clear idea of what you expect to happen.

2. *The Employer's Goal in Negotiating:* You will find out what many of the company's goals are only when you are already in negotiation. Some of them are already known to you, or at least you can make reasonable assumptions. Put yourself in your employer's place and try to discover what she expects from the session. Any hints you get prior to the session puts you ahead.

3. *Areas of Agreement:* Before the session, and especially during it, try to decide what areas you both can agree on. Is the salary offer acceptable? What other conditions put forward are more or less acceptable? Which ones are not? Which ones can be discussed further and which ones, if any, are nonnegotiable? (You will definitely not manage the Baghdad office!) The aim here is to let

the company's negotiator meet his goals completely, or at least in part, while you meet yours. How can this be done? Once you settle on all the goals you both agree on, all that remains are those you don't agree on. Now comes the hard part!

4. *Reconciliation of Goals:* The art of successful negotiation is to come away with both sides winning because both bent their goals a bit to accommodate the other side until a compromise was fashioned. Be prepared to give away something in order to get something in return that you consider more important. If the employers will not meet the salary you want, ask for it in the form of a performance bonus, based on your promise to do certain things by a certain date. Or perhaps they will shorten the waiting period for your first raise to satisfy your requirement. At this point they want to hire you, have already decided you are the one, and will not let you walk out unhappy or not taking the job, unless there is no other way out. You must provide them that way out. You may assume they will make every effort to meet your reasonable requests (no demands here).

Create an Atmosphere of Trust

Negotiations will succeed only if there is an atmosphere of mutual trust. By the time you get to this final stage, you have had at least a limited chance to create it. In your meetings with your potential employers, no matter how high or low the level of the person, be open and frank. Be polite to everyone. You can foster trust on their part by always being good-natured in your dealings, accommodating to their needs, and sociable.

In your negotiations, you want to have them perceive your honesty, which is a requirement before trust can be granted. You cannot simply proclaim that you are honest, but you can imply it by showing your honesty in your dealings with other people.* Find some interesting examples in which your honesty played a role and, without seeming obvious about it, try to work them into the discussion.

---

* As Ralph Waldo Emerson said, "The more he proclaimed his honesty, the more we counted the silverware."

When it appears that the negotiations are over, it's up to you to activate the agreement. You can do this by a simple "Thank you!" Shake hands all around (if others are present), thank each person by name, and tell them how much you're looking forward to working with them.

You have just been hired. Congratulations!

Now, go out and party! You deserve a celebration!

Hired Again . . . Hallelujah!

22

They like you . . . they really, really like you! They proved it by hiring you! They brought you in from the cold and gave you another chance. It didn't matter to them that you were fired from your last job, and they just *loved* your résumé. There is justice, after all. But you aren't coming into this job with the same naïve attitude you had at the last place. Oh, no . . . no way! You've been down to the firing squad and don't intend to make any mistakes this time that could lead to a repeat of *that* humiliating disaster.

Realize you have been traumatized by your firing and, like it or not, will bear the psychological scars for a long time. Susan W. loved every minute of her first day on the new job. It was a dream come true . . . until, a few minutes before she left for the day, her new boss stuck his head out of his office and said, "Will you come in here for a minute? There's something we need to talk about." Her heart dropped into her shoes, and she broke into a cold sweat and started trembling, ready to burst into tears. She had been fired from her previous job at the same time of the day, and when her ex-boss broke the news to her just before she went home, her nightmare began with those exact words.

As she entered her new employer's office she didn't realize how untenable her reaction was. How could she be fired from her new job on the very first day? Her boss shoved an open box of candy in her direction and gave her a printed invitation to the office picnic, to be held that weekend. "It's a good way to get to know a lot of people here, and I thought it would be nice if you could come. Can you?" He looked at her solicitously. She felt like hugging him or screaming with joy, but she just nodded and said, "Oh, thank you. Thank you."

Realize that you have been traumatized, and the emotions can be set off at any time by trigger words or acts with entirely different meanings. Recognizing the problem will not erase the trauma you've been through, nor the instinctive reactions that ensue. However, you'll be able to deal with them effectively if you know they may recur. Gradually the stimuli will fade away as you gain more self-confidence. But the residue they leave can serve a useful purpose. Your firing sensitized you in positive ways as well as negative ways. From now on you'll have a constant awareness of danger signs and your former naïveté will be tempered with reality. (Been there, done that!) Being sensitized to conditions that could lead to a repeat arms you to forestall or prevent them again entirely, insofar as the situation may be under your control to influence.

From now on you will keep, *at home,* an up-to-date list of your network and cultivate it so these individuals are available when you need them. From now on you will photocopy your Rolodex file at least once a year and keep the copy at home. From now on you will *always* be open to calls from executive recruiters, always keep an ear out for new job openings that could advance your career, and always be prepared to leave your job at a moment's notice. Don't misinterpret this as advocating disloyalty to your firm. But you owe loyalty first to yourself. If you do your job well, give it your best efforts—your responsibility to your employer ends there. That may not be the way it is in novels, but that's how it is in life.

So, what to do? The first thing to do is nothing. Just relax, be yourself, and let things happen. Your first day, your first week, your first month on the job you will be noticed, and you will notice things. Put a smile on your face and let everyone know how happy you are to be there. Don't make any close friends yet. That can come later, when you've had a chance to find out who's who. Neither should you be aloof, lest you be branded a snob. Your initial period on the job is a short honeymoon. The regulars have all heard about you, and most of them will be solicitous and eager to help you get to know the ropes. The atmosphere will be supportive.

Learn what's expected of you. You may already know your mission in this new company. Take a little time, though, to go around and introduce yourself and meet people. Talk to old-timers, the mailroom staff, and secretaries as well as senior management and your colleagues in your department and elsewhere. They have worthwhile things to tell you, and you'll expand your contact base further as well as your knowledge of the company and its procedures.

This is a great time to do this. Later on you'll have no reason to, or no time for it. Now, you'll find everybody helpful, eager to start the new hiree out on the right foot. Listen to their stories, their gossip—but don't take sides on any issues. Ask them to tell you what their job is and how they work with your department, what they expect of you and of your department. This will give you a good, basic knowledge of the company and start you off right. Ask a lot of questions, listen carefully to the answers, and at the end of the day write a little journal of the important things you learned and the people you met.

Give yourself a goal. Ask yourself what you want to do in the first year here, then narrow it down to the first month. What is your mission, your task? Write it down and, if you're a bit uncertain, confide in the person who hired you and see if she agrees. Then find out what your new company sees as its mission and its goal in the corporate world it moves in. What does your company want to accomplish? Drop by the public relations department and get copies of any brochures, annual reports, or other material describing the company and study them. Once you have these definitions, ask yourself if you have enough knowledge and training to accomplish the company's goals. If not, will you be able to get it as you work? You might need a course or two at an educational institution. Some companies have their own training facility, and you may qualify for it. These inquiries will not only result in your acquiring knowledge crucial to your getting ahead and useful for the rest of your career, but will label you as a go-getter—not a bad way to start a new job.

Some people in today's work force have a conflict between their desire to "be me" and the conformist atmosphere in the average corporation.

The modern company is an organism, a team of people working toward individual and corporate goals. By the very nature of a corporation or company, no matter how large or small, it's necessary to submerge your individualism, at least outwardly, for the good of the company's mission and the efficient completion of your task and that of the others. Only a few industries actively encourage individual expression, such as fashion, film, and advertising. And even in those industries there's plenty of conformity in different guises.

Some companies have relaxed attitudes and expectations of what they consider good corporate behavior in manner as well as dress. IBM was once so rigid that an IBM employee could be identified in a crowd as easily as a zebra in a herd of sheep. Today IBM has a more relaxed attitude, realizing that the new generation's way of conforming is to look different.

Men with earrings and women with tattoos are still rare on boards of directors, but at least the possibility exists today. If neon-dyed hair and outré apparel are your way of self-expression, you ought to rethink your appearance if you want to get ahead. If you simply cannot, or will not, conform to corporate custom in dress and behavior, you must ask yourself if the corporate environment is really for you.

Observe how others in similar positions in the company dress and take a look one level up in the management chain. Dressing one level higher is safe in most places—a way to signal your intentions to get ahead. But don't dress any higher than that. You don't want to be the only one who dresses just like the boss, or perhaps better. Take inventory of your wardrobe. Have repairs made, buttons resewed, zippers replaced, everything dry-cleaned. Get rid of threadbare clothing, and, if necessary, buy one or two new outfits. Before you wear any questionable outfit to work, wait a while. After a few weeks you'll know if it's appropriate.

Stay with it. Make good grooming, tasteful attire, and personal hygiene a priority. Be consistent. Unlike books, corporate citizens are often judged by their covers. There's a Japanese saying, "The nail that sticks up will be hammered down." It's true to some degree here as well, no matter how laid-back the corporate environment may seem outwardly. Watch the decision makers and take your cues from them.

You'll Never Get Fired in This Town Again

23

It won't help you if you've just been fired; however, in a few years you can create enough security to be able to support yourself for six months to a year, then two years, if you lose your job again. Then, sooner than you think, you'll be on the road to true financial independence. Wouldn't it be wonderful if you didn't have to depend on a salary for your livelihood and never again suffer the humiliation of being fired? There are several ways to reach this happy goal. Job security no longer comes from jobs—it flows from the financial security that comes from either working for yourself or from the coming to fruition of a powerful plan to accumulate enough wealth to live on independently. The first level of such a plan is to accumulate enough savings to support yourself until you get your next job. The final level is to accumulate enough wealth so that you'll never need to work for someone else again unless you want to. Wouldn't that be a nice thing to be remembered for by your children? It's time-consuming and it isn't easy, but isn't it worth the effort if real security is yours in the end?

The two surest ways of not being fired are (1) start your own business, and (2) achieve financial independence in stages. The first method may not be for the fainthearted. The second method requires time, patience, and willpower. If you think that you're just an average person with an average salary (when you have one) and that you have no "big idea" that will bring you wealth, so what's the use of even trying—think again. With application, perseverance, and a bit of luck, anyone can do it. Luck is what happens when preparation meets opportunity. You can make your own luck if you start preparing for it now. How many times have you heard it said of someone who became rich, "She was lucky!"? That's the excuse of a loser. You're already lucky. You live in a country where it's possible to become, if not rich, at least comfortable enough to live off your savings and interest. It's not as hopeless as the losers think it is—the ones who gave up before they even started.

If you want to grab the brass ring of financial success, you first have to invest in the admission fee to the carousel, get up on the horse, and go around in circles for a while before you get the opportunity to reach for it. Just do it, goes today's credo.

Starting Your Own Business

Many businesses were started by accident. I met a fine gentleman a few years ago who had sold his company, a janitorial service, when he retired. How he started the business is worth telling. During the Great Depression of 1929 he was a high school student and worked part time in his father's haberdashery in Los Angeles. Not having anything to do one day, he decided to clean, really clean, the front of the store, including the sidewalk, so it would be attractive and induce customers to come into the store.

Being young and inexperienced, he didn't know the proper way to do things, so he innovated where he couldn't find out how it was done. First he swept and hosed off the sidewalk. Then he got some gasoline and carefully scraped and wiped off every glob of chewing gum that had bonded onto the sidewalk over the years. In order to get the now-mottled sidewalk back into some kind of uniform appearance, he made a witches' brew of hot water, bleach, ammonia, and scouring powder and scrubbed every inch of the sidewalk with a wire brush until the original color of the concrete reappeared, the first time it had been seen since the building was erected! Then he went to work on the brass fittings on the outside of the store until they shone like gold, the awning over the display windows, and the windows themselves. He bought some gold and black paint and freshened up the signs on the store and then went inside the display windows and gave them a thorough going over.

By this time he had attracted the attention of the neighboring store-keepers on either side of his father's store. By comparison, their once-comparable storefronts and sidewalks now looked shabby, and they wanted him to do the same for them. He obliged—for a small fee. Gradually word got around and he was soon so busy that he had to hire some friends to help him clean all the stores that wanted his services. (You can see what's coming by now.) He borrowed a truck from an uncle, put a sign on its sides, printed flyers, and went around the neighborhood giving them out to all the businesses. Within a few years he had his own business with a dozen full-time employees and built it up from there into a major local company serving a wide area. He created his fortune out of nothing but imagination, guts, a little help from his friends and relatives, and a lot of hard work. The wonder of America is that there are still opportunities like this all over the country. What stops many people from exploiting them is false pride, sloth, lack of imagination, and all the other excuses we give ourselves as to why it won't work for us.

Most people lack the nerve to risk going into business. I did. My wife and I were tricked into taking over a failed travel agency by the promises of a promoter who guaranteed to back us financially and bring us lots of business. After we had signed the contract and put up our little invest-ment, he backed out (when we insisted on keeping our promises to the seller), leaving us holding the bag for his portion of the down payment. "Someday you'll thank me," he said as he took off. I would never have believed it that day, but in hindsight he was right. We were forced to make a success of our situation or lose our investment and possibly face a law-suit, and so we did, often taking no salary for weeks at a time in order to pay the employees. Meeting the payroll is the rite of passage for all entre-preneurs. The financial independence we enjoy today is partly the result of the promoter's betrayal. (The moral here is something about today's enemies becoming tomorrow's friends.) Left to our own devices we prob-ably would have talked ourselves out of it and opted for the continued false security of salaried jobs.

It helps if there is an entrepreneur in your family, a parent or other close relative. Eighty percent of today's new small businesses have an entrepreneur in the family. There are many risks to being in business. Risk is the price you pay for success. It's no bungee jump—if you fail, nothing will pull you back at the last second. The stakes are even higher if others depend on your ability to make a living. So your first step to financial independence should be to turn inward, analyze your personal situation, and evaluate what will happen to those you love if you fail. Talk it over with them, especially if they will be involved in the risk. Discuss it with friends you trust, preferably those already in business. A thousand dumb questions are better than one stupid mistake, so be absolutely certain that you really want to explore this option to financial independence before you go further.

Should you become a consultant? A wag once described a consultant as "someone looking for a job." There is a temptation to go into consultancy, especially if you've built up a body of good, useable knowledge. You can work your own hours, you tell yourself, and maybe pull down those big consulting fees you've heard about. Certainly, if you're out of work and have a chance to do some consulting, take it. It might even lead you into your next job. But think carefully before committing to this as a career. Most such consultancies wither on the vine while waiting for the next client and don't last longer than a year or so. Spend your energy trying to get another job with a steady salary instead of a client who will be gone in a few weeks along with his checkbook.

Are You an Entrepreneur by Nature?

To thine own self be true.

—Shakespeare, Hamlet

Every little boy and girl, when they are about eleven years old, have a plan for their lives. They know what they want to be when they grow up. As we mature some of us realize that dream of the long-ago child. Those are the fortunate ones. Most of us realize as adults that the dreams of our childhood are . . . well, childish. We slowly let go of our fantasies and adopt the "sensible" materialistic trappings of society and the demands of reality. And yet, within many people toiling anonymously in the bowels of large corporations, an entrepreneur waits to emerge, but is usually kept back by those two great censors, conformity and fear. It's easier to go to work every day, earn our keep, enjoy the material things of life, and divert ourselves in the many ways offered by our rich culture.

A firing blows our internal fuses and gives our hidden child the opportunity it has waited for. Most of the time we manage to get the little tot of memory back into his box where he belongs. But sometimes we listen— and act. Thus is born, from a humiliating firing, another entrepreneur. This unique urge to be one's own boss is not created; entrepreneurs are born and know it at an early age. Are you an entrepreneur?

The original meaning of the word *career* was *racehorse:* swift, free, and in headlong forward motion. While that also describes an out-of-control automobile it has generally come to mean one's life work, if not a dedication, at least a gainful occupation that adds something to society while it enriches its owner monetarily and spiritually. A successful career is the embodiment of an ideal that often begins in childhood. Every child dreams of someday having a career in (fill in the blank: aerospace, medicine, fashion?). That our dreams often turn sour when subjected to the whims of fate is illustrated by an incident in *The Honeymooners,* the classic Jackie Gleason television sitcom. Gleason's character, Ralph Kramden, works as a city bus driver. In one episode, he runs into an old rival and learns that he has become a huge success in the manufacturing business. When asked what he does for a living, Ralph says that he "runs things" at the bus company (an aggrandizement that escalates into his being the boss of the company). The denouement comes when Ralph finally admits to being a bus driver—and his friend to being an assistant plumber!

The incident illustrates a profound truth about human nature and, like many of Gleason's skits, deftly skewers them with hilarious results. The burger flipper down at the neighborhood fast-food franchise does not believe he is fulfilling his ideal career as he constructs the company's ten-billionth burger. He dreams of owning his own franchise one day. Or perhaps he's saving up for college or wants to be known as a musician, a basketball player, or a rocket scientist. He aspires to a real career that will bring him money, recognition, approval, and fulfillment. The college students emerging from graduation ceremonies on campus clutching their diplomas have memories of four wonderful college years in their heads and certification of their expertise in their hands. Now they can begin their careers. Everything before was prelude. Now their real life begins, they think. It starts with a career.

We seek careers because they are guarantors of success, financial security, eventual financial independence, and the respect of one's peers. If an institutionalized career track is not what you want and you're unhappy in dead-end jobs, perhaps your career lies in business ownership.

Being fired indicates that you may have an entrepreneurial streak. Perhaps you aren't a corporate animal and your ex-employers discovered it before you did. If so, they may have done you a favor by firing you and forcing you to face reality. That is, provided you have the good sense to realize who you are and what you really should be doing with your life, and the courage to do something about it.

This is especially true if you've been fired from a small to medium-sized (500 or fewer employees) company. People used to working in huge corporations with their cushiony benefits and remoteness from the daily risks of a small business usually have a more difficult time on their own. If you're not a couch potato and prefer to play competitive sports rather than watch from the sidelines as others play, you may be an entrepreneurial type. Are you what the ads call a self-starter? Do you have trouble sitting still because you have so much energy? When you were a child did you collect cans and bottles for the refund, try your hand at a corner lemonade stand, have a paper route, sell Girl Scout cookies?

Are you fed up with endless committees, memos, meetings, and all the other consensus-building, time-wasting, and refusal-to-try-new-ideas atmospherics of a large corporation?

Joe S. works for a railroad. I once asked him about putting brochure racks in each compartment on the trains to promote tours to see the U.S.A. When he expressed unwillingness, I asked why. "If you were doing it, you'd go to a store, buy some racks, hire a carpenter or handyman, and have them up in the trains in a few days," he said. "Not here. The first thing we'd do is appoint a committee to study the idea's feasibility. Then we'd do a cost analysis, environmental impact study, and all the rest. If the idea eventually got approved, we'd appoint a design committee to work out a design for the racks and have them fabricated in our workshops. A team would be assembled to install them, which could take months, depending on schedules and availability of equipment. The whole process would take six months to a year or more, provided some bureaucrat didn't kill the whole plan somewhere along the way. Are you getting the idea yet?" If you're rolling your eyes at this point, perhaps you are an entrepreneurial type.

Are you a nonconformist, stubborn when you think you're right but willing to acknowledge and change when you may be wrong? Do you like to keep your own counsel, know that the shortest distance between two points is not necessarily what the manual says it is, have creative tendencies and an urge to succeed? Do you sometimes daydream about your ideal career... what you *really* want to do? Would you be willing to act on it ... make the break? Are you bored with your present career? Do you have an urge to bring others along, give them a boost up? Are you good at teaching and instructing others, a natural supervisor of projects? Do you secretly resent working for others? If that describes you, perhaps it's time to throw off the corporate insecurity blanket and test the waters.

Are You too Young or too Old?

Age is a consideration, but not decisive if you are determined. Hollywood's child moguls, Silicon Valley's twenty-something innovators, many barely past adolescence when their star ascended, created a baseline of age and lowered the barriers. At the other end, Colonel Sanders started his business when he was sixty-two. Although most new entrepreneurs are typically in their early thirties, there's no hard and fast rule about age. If you think you can do it and have the energy, the rest of the problems are usually solvable. What determines the success of a new venture is not the age, social standing, or ethnic background of the entrepreneur or any of a dozen other reasons. What sinks new businesses are problems such as not having enough capital, poor planning, and poor management skills. If you can overcome these, you're on your way, regardless of where you come from and what your background is.

Don't confuse changing jobs with changing careers or becoming an entrepreneur. You can change jobs by getting a different job in the same industry. Changing careers may mean getting another job, but this time in a field different from the one you worked in previously. You may still be on the salary track and subject to the ups and downs of a salaried job. Becoming an entrepreneur means trading the regular paycheck and the sense of security of corporate life for the unreliable (but potentially larger) rewards of your own business and the insecurity of owning a business. But this trade-off has a huge advantage over the corporate life. If you succeed, you'll be free in a sense that you can never find in a salaried job. You will be fully in charge of your ship, the captain of your soul, and that is something so exciting and wonderful it defies description. You'll be your own person, self-made and proud.

Inventory Your Skills and Assets

Are you good with math? Do you have an understanding of bookkeeping and accounting? Are you creative, always innovating new ideas and ways to do things? Are you a people-person, who enjoys people and solving their problems? Think of all the things you like to do and equate them with the skills you might need in your own business. Write it all down and look at it. Then make a list of all the things you think are needed in a person to succeed in business. Compare the lists. Show them to a mentor or a business friend for comments. This exercise will rough out the outlines of the business environment you might be happy in. For example, if you like to talk with people, you may enjoy owning a business that caters to the needs of people, such as a retail store, a travel agency, or another business that deals with the public. Or you may prefer to work alone. If you combine this with a good head for bookkeeping, perhaps a billing service is for you. Slowly you define who you are, what your skills are, and then cast about for a business that combines them.*

Testing Your Business Skills

If you don't know where to begin, consider taking a skills evaluation test. Contact your local department of human resources, the state employment department, or your nearest college or university, or check out the subject in the public library reference department or on the Internet. There are seminars for this purpose, and this may be a good start as you cast about for ideas.

Unless you already know what you want to do and have already developed thoughts on the subject, this is a step you should not take lightly.

---

*Insider's Tip for Women: *For information about opportunities specifically for women going into their own business, or the women's workplace in general, contact the following: Catalyst for Women, Inc., Information Center, 250 Park Avenue South, 5th Floor, New York, NY 10003-1459 (telephone 212/777-8900); Mother's Home Business Network, P.O. Box 423, East Meadow, NY 11590 (telephone 516/997-7394); and the Association of Enterprising Mothers, 6965 El Camino Real, Suite 105-612, Carlsbad, CA 92009 (telephone 619/434-9225, or 800/223-9260).*

Think of skills assessment as the road map of your future. Before you embark on this new venture, before it's too late to change your mind, you'd better be certain that you have at least the rudimentary skills for what you want to do. The technical training or special education you may need for various businesses can be acquired later, either in a training course or on the job itself—experience is a good teacher. But your willingness to persevere until you reach your goal can be seriously undermined if you discover too late that this is really not your cup of tea and maybe you should have chosen another business or stayed back in the corporate environment. Businesses are not like jobs. Once in them, they're impossible to quit like a job or to walk away from without serious consequences. A mistake in judgment at this time can become a costly blunder later on.

Selecting the Right Business

Your next step is to choose the business to be in. The Small Business Administration, your local chamber of commerce, and the business section of your library are all good sources of information. If you have some money but no special skills, you may opt to purchase a franchise with a proven track record. This provides a full turn-key operation and just about guarantees success. However, the cost of buying into a successful franchise is high. You also are constrained to operate within rigid procedures and usually must buy your supplies from the franchiser or its recommended firms. There may be other problems that you're not aware of when you attend the rose-colored-glasses seminar held by the franchiser to entice you to invest in his sure-thing franchise.

In a case still being appealed, a 1990 Bankruptcy Court ruling that awarded $2.8 million in damages to Vylene Green, a restaurant franchisee, has recently been upheld by a higher court.[1] In the case, Green contended that the chain opened another outlet only 1.4 miles away from her business. Her attorney contended that the chain engaged in a pattern of opening company-owned stores close to its franchise operators. If you opt for a franchise business, be certain to talk to owners of other franchises of the same company and to explore offerings of other chains. Perhaps you can become wealthy with some franchise operations, but you could also lose your investment and buy into a lot of problems you didn't plan on.

Many small independent businesses that are not doing well can be jolted into success by a new owner who works hard and brings creative approaches to problems. You may have a special skill or be able to identify a need in the market that no one is meeting.

New developments in technology are bringing new opportunities for entrepreneurs. Don't listen to pessimists. Let your head teach you, but follow your heart and do what you're convinced is right for you. If you don't, for the rest of your life you'll have that nagging feeling of what might have been. If you try and fail, at least you know you did your best. But even if you fail the first time, you may be bitten by the entrepreneurial bug and want to keep on until you succeed. Persistence is more important than luck in determining success in a business.

Now more than ever the climate is right for entrepreneurs. If you are a woman, it may encourage you to know that women in America own more than four and a half million businesses and start new ones at twice the rate of men. Opportunities abound for the handicapped, immigrants, and other minorities as well. That doesn't mean it's going to be easy, but the gates are wider and entry into new businesses has never been more accessible.

How to Achieve Financial Independence

If you never give up, you can make anything work.

—William O'Neill, NASA Galileo Project Manager, as quoted in the *Los Angeles Times,* July 14, 1996

What follows is only a guide, a suggested route to financial independence. The steps recommended will, if followed with perseverance, lead toward financial security and eliminate reliance on a steady salary when the plan matures. All cases are different, and each person should tailor the plan to his or her individual needs. However, this should not become an excuse to water down the plan to the point where it ceases to be effective. We are sometimes our own worst enemies!

A wise man once said that to achieve success you must think like an ant but act like a grasshopper. He was paraphrasing the fable of the grasshopper and the ant, in which the grasshopper spends the summer hopping around having fun, while the industrious ant just keeps plugging away, putting more and more food into his nest. When winter comes, of course, the grasshopper starves while the ant has all the food he needs. Applied to your quest for financial independence you must think like the ant, but in your career you should act, at least at times, like the grasshopper. From time to time you must make a leap, to another job, to more responsibility, to further your career. This will in turn reinforce the ant part of your plan, which is to set as much money aside as you possibly can against the time you will finally no longer need a job to survive. Then you can truly live like the carefree grasshopper, only now you'll be hopping around the world on vacations and having a permanent good time.

Unless a rich aunt leaves you her fortune or you win the lottery, you'll have to achieve financial independence the old-fashioned way—by earning it. Like the oyster that slowly creates the pearl, attaining freedom from being fired takes time. But it can come surprisingly early if you have a plan and stick to it. Right now you've just been fired and the last thing you are thinking about is financial independence, except in your daydreams. What you need is a job. But soon you'll have one and a new and perhaps better income stream. Unless you want to risk a repeat of the humiliation you just went through, you'd better begin to attack the problem.

Just as you regularly make your life insurance, your car insurance, and other necessary insurance payments, so should you pay your job insurance bill. Unfortunately, no company offers such a plan, and unemployment insurance, godsend though it is, doesn't last long and doesn't pay much to begin with. What you need is a job insurance plan that will keep you going in more or less the same lifestyle until you get another job, no matter how long it may take. You'll have to self-insure—do it yourself. Here's how:

The Only Job Insurance You Can Depend On

Take your first paycheck on your new job, deduct and bank ten percent, and live on the rest as if what's left is your actual salary. You can do it. If you can live on your present salary, you can get by on ten percent less (see "Tithe Yourself," below, for details). It may take a little planning, a little sacrificing, but unless your salary is equal to the minimum wage you won't miss it. Make it 15 percent if you can—20 percent would be wonderful. If you're not certain you have the willpower to keep this up month after month, ask your new employer if he can arrange for it to be deducted from your salary before you even see it and banked for you. The less you have to think about it, the less tempting it will be to dip into it.

Set savings goals! When your account reaches $1,000, pull it out of the low-interest bank account, leaving in a little to keep the account going, and invest the money in a high-income mutual fund, where you'll find returns of eight to ten percent not uncommon. Then let your bank account fill up again to the next goal line. Your first major milepost in your insurance-against-being-fired plan should be $10,000. Impossible? Not at all. You'll be there sooner than you think, and from there, you're well on the way to complete financial security and independence.

Let's say that your survival salary (the least amount of money you'll need to get along for an entire year if you're out of work) is $30,000. (Fill in the figures that make sense for your needs, but be conservative.) To cover expenses for six months you'll need $15,000. When you have saved the first $10,000 you'll have saved almost enough to survive for the six-month period, and you will have already progressed one third of the way to your one-year survival goal of $30,000. At the rate you decide to save, figure how long it will take you to get to the $10,000 level. A year? Two years? Three? Now you see the timeline beginning to emerge. Your job is to find out how to shorten it so that you can get there sooner.

Make it a game. When you realize the importance of the goal to your life, it will become a challenge. Once your long-range goals have been reached you will forever be out of danger, not only of suffering the humiliation of another firing, but you'll be within sight of never having to have to work for a living again! Surely a goal like that is worth the candle, worth a bit of sacrifice, a little belt-tightening now so that you can enjoy it later, for the rest of your life. As the money begins to fill your coffers, the phenomenon of reinvestment of dividends becomes more and more powerful and you begin to get the first twinges of financial security as you watch your nest egg get bigger and bigger—slowly at first, then faster and faster.

If you stick with the plan and resist the temptation to buy a new car, for example, when the old one can go on for a few more years, you'll eventually find that $100,000 is within reach. Perhaps it's not yet within your grasp, but it will be out there, getting closer.

Be ingenious and creative in your efforts to add more to your nest egg as quickly as you can so that you can get over the tedious beginning period and get into advanced savings. Perhaps you have a hobby that can make some money for you. Consider taking some part-time work, even a second job if you can handle the physical and time constraints that it will put on you. If you live on ten percent less than your main salary and also have a second job, you can bank the entire second salary. If you're married but do not yet have children, consider banking all, or a major part, of your spouse's salary. If you and your spouse can agree to the sacrifice, consider both taking two jobs, at least for a while. If you live on one salary, that means that you can bank the other three! You will rapidly accelerate your savings plans in this manner. While you're young and vigorous, it's an option to consider. Most people are lazy and content to go along the salary track, slow but steady, to eventual retirement. If you put the sacrifice into your life early, you'll be retired years before they can even consider it.

While you're looking for a new job, study the plan outlined here. It worked for me, and in one variation or another, for hundreds of thousands of other people. It will work for you if you follow it rigorously. But you need to make a few lifestyle changes. Just as you go to the health club and work hard on the machines to become fit, you can apply the same tenacity to accumulating financial muscle that you apply to the Stairmaster or the treadmill. It may sound hopeless as you gaze at your bills and wonder how you'll pay them now that you're out of work, but you will quickly be past this point. Start now! Sooner than you think you'll be able to tell them what to do with their job. There are things you can begin doing now to put yourself on the road to financial independence and real wealth, even if you're not yet working again.

Get Credit Cards Under Control

The popular wisdom is that credit cards, like demon rum, are the first step down the rocky road to sin, degradation, and financial ruin. Indeed, many people spend themselves into bankruptcy by profligate and irresponsible use of the colorful little cards. But, then, many people drive recklessly and cause automobile accidents. Is that any reason not to drive? Credit cards, like other modern conveniences, are a wonderful financial tool when used correctly and with discipline. When used otherwise they're the fool's ticket to ruin. What trips up the novice is the Las Vegas effect.

When you're in Las Vegas and buy a roll of chips, they are suddenly transformed from real, hard-earned dollars into play dough. Colorful and small, like credit cards, they suddenly lose their serious link to the grim world of commerce. Once seen thus, they are easy and tempting to use. It isn't money you are losing, it's just a gaudy, easily replaced toy, like the phony money in a game of Monopoly. Or so it seems until the time comes to return to the real world.

The same phenomenon occurs with credit cards. It's no accident that they are small, friendly-looking, and easy to obtain. Almost every mail brings news from some bank in Ohio or Iowa that has a fabulous deal on credit cards for you. You shift into a feel-good mood of fantasy and spend as if it was play money—until the day to reckon up arrives, as it always does.

But used properly, they can save money and shortcut your trip to independence. First, get rid of all but one card. There's no reason to have a dozen credit cards for gas stations, department stores, and generic charge cards. It may give you a false sense of importance and security to have all those cards in your wallet and get all that mail every month, but it's causing money to seep out of your life, money you desperately need to meet your goal of financial independence. Just scissor them all but the one you want to keep. Select a card that's in general use everywhere, such as MasterCard or Visa. Get one that gives you airline mileage (forget about their points for catalog items; airline miles are valuable and useful while the catalog "gifts" are no bargains—you can get better deals at your local department or discount store) and tell the company you will stay with them, or sign up, if they waive the annual fee. They may not, but a surprising number of the big companies will.* Use the remaining credit card for everything you purchase from now on, if you can. Each purchase you make with a credit card instead of check saves a little more money for

---

*Warning: *Read the fine print in the sales prospectus. Don't accept the card unless it offers a one-month period of grace before interest rates are charged. Some companies charge interest from the day you make a purchase with the card! The big ones usually charge interest only after a thirty-day grace period. Reject any card that doesn't offer this grace period or your card will become a liability and not an asset. If you have any doubts, call their "800" number and verify it. You want two things from your credit card: (1) a thirty-day grace period, and (2) airline mileage. If you don't get both, find a card company that offers them. Recently some card issuers began penalizing users who pay off their balance before interest rates can be charged. Ask about this before you select the card to use, and if so, go to another company with a better attitude toward people who pay their bills on time.*

you because you avoid nickel and dime check charges and bank fees and you pay your credit card bill once a month with one check, one envelope (which they provide), and one postage stamp.

"Many a mickle makes a muckle," said Scottish poet Robert Burns, by which he meant that a lot of seemingly insignificant savings, when added up, can accumulate into a formidable amount over time. With credit card use the trick is to *pay the bill as soon after it arrives as you can in order to avoid the high monthly interest charges.* Once you pass the one-month credit period and have to pay interest on what you owe, you begin to lose. If you cannot meet the payments before interest charges are levied, get rid of all of your cards because they'll become a problem instead of an asset.

The three major disadvantages of using credit cards are (1) they don't seem like real money, (2) the temptation is strong to buy unnecessary things, and (3) interest charges. If you can discipline yourself to avoid unnecessary purchases and if you pay the monthly bill within the grace period, you're on your way to making the cards work for you instead of vice versa.

Use your credit card prudently. Use it to buy only the things you absolutely need. Something with the power to blow you right into insolvency (if you let it) needs to be handled with care, respect, and thought. It may seem like play money—a harmless chip of colorful plastic. Like many powerful things, used wrongly it can cause misery and destruction. But used properly it can be a fine tool to help you on your way to financial independence. Use it at the supermarket, pay your utility bills with it if the company permits, use it for every purchase you can think of and with every company that accepts it. Use it all the time—but use it *only to buy necessities and nothing else!* And *pay the bill the day you receive it, before interest is charged.* That's the real secret.

Adopt a More Frugal Lifestyle

Which of these statements are true?

- I will live forever.
- If I smoke, I will not get cancer.
- If I don't start to save money now it's not important because I'll be able to start as soon as (fill in your excuse here).

You see how preposterous it is that you have not yet begun to plan for financial independence? Start today! It will conserve valuable funds you need to live on if you start today, while you're still unemployed. Examine your lifestyle and how you spend your money. Have a financial advisor help you if you feel at a loss. Here are six things you can do immediately:

1. Cut down on the number of times you eat out each month. Eat out not more than once a week unless you have a social obligation. In that case, skip your other restaurant meals and eat at home. Polish up your kitchen skills. A good cookbook will pay for itself the first time you use it and will give you a lot of pleasure as well. Choose a moderately priced restaurant for dining out, and if you like a glass of wine in the evening, enjoy one at home before the meal, rather than adding an expensive glass of wine to the restaurant bill. Once you get into the "frugal gourmet" frame of mind you'll discover dozens of ways to save a little money without cutting into your enjoyment of the dining experience.

2. Buy food more economically—use cheaper cuts of meat and less expensive fish. A little garlic and spice and creative cooking can turn a humble pound of ground beef or some inexpensive red snapper into a sumptuous treat.

3. Buy staples like toilet paper in bulk.

4. Use coupons, but only for things you would normally buy anyhow.

5. Buy the specials, the weekly bargains.

6. Buy good-quality clothing, but concentrate on mix and match so you don't need a lot of different outfits. Stay away from overpriced designer brands. Find the outlet stores in your town and shop them for bargains. A friend of ours buys all her clothing at a certain charity rummage store. She finds exquisite dresses and other clothing donated by wealthy people who paid full price for them. Our friend always looks well dressed and sports the best labels in town. Are you too proud to buy a bargain just because it's from an outlet or charity store?

Get Rid of Car Payments

You'll have time for that expensive car after you save the money for it and accomplish your goals under your plan for financial independence. In the meantime, drive a reliable used car and keep it in good repair so it gets you around town. If you need a new car once in a while to take a trip, for example, consider renting one or use other forms of transportation. Monthly payments on a new car will make a mockery of budgets. Run the figures on your car loan and you'll discover that you're paying for the car twice over, and more, on a typical loan. Here is one way to look at it: If your dream car is, say, $30,000, that amount in a safe, high-income mutual fund could generate around $2,500 to $3,000 per year in interest, and that's only in the first year. It compounds rapidly.*

Have your car serviced regularly. The secret of long motor life is regular oil changes and proper fluid levels in the transmission, brakes, etc. Whether you change oil every 3,000 miles as custom dictates, or follow the new recommendations in *Consumers Report* for twice that mileage, or more, do it without fail, and your engine should run trouble free if you're lucky. Corner slowly and drive at moderate speeds, even on the express roads, and you will decrease wear and tear on the vehicle and prolong its life. Today's engines will last a long time if properly maintained, and it's not uncommon to drive a car for over 150,000 miles before it wears out. Even then, a complete motor overhaul (rebuilt motor) in a car with no other major problems will cost around $3,000—a lot cheaper than a new car. Unless you are mechanically inclined and can fix your own car, you're at the mercy of repair shops. Try to find a good, small repair shop that specializes in your vehicle. Word of mouth is about the only way to find them, but they're worth the search. There are still good, honest, and reasonably priced repair shops if you look long enough.

Your automobile is the second-largest purchase (the first is your house) you will make. But unless your vehicle becomes a collector's item your money is gone when the car's life is over, whereas your home is an investment that will create wealth for you over time. The secret of not losing

---

*If you have that much money in the bank, or even somewhat less, dedicate one year's worth of interest to buying a transportation car for a few thousand dollars. This preserves your hard-earned principal and lets it keep on compounding for you. Invest the $30,000 in a new car and you lose twice: the money is gone forever in a rapidly declining asset (the new car), and you are out thousands of dollars in interest that it could have been earning for you if you left it in the fund and drew out only the interest.

money on cars is proper maintenance and prolonging the life of the car as long as possible.

Tithe Yourself

Charity begins at home. Before you give donations to causes you believe in, give (save) to your home-based charity first.[†] This step, along with the more frugal lifestyle you adopt, is crucial to your financial independence. When you once again have a steady salary, take ten percent of each paycheck (fifteen or even twenty percent is better and will get you to your goal faster, but ten percent—and no less—will do the job) and invest it regularly—that means from each and every paycheck, no matter how tempting it might be not to—in an aggressive growth corporate stock fund with a good mutual fund company. There are dozens of established, reliable companies to chose from. Check out the annual mutual fund issue of *U.S. News and World Report* magazine (or any of the many other sources that regularly evaluate funds) for ideas on which companies to consider. Yes, of course there is some risk. But the history of the stock market shows that good stocks, intelligently chosen, and held for the long term, always do well for the investor. If you're investing with a large, well-established fund with a good track record and the particular fund you chose is identified by the fund company as low risk, your risk will usually be confined to getting a lower rate than you thought you might.

What is risky is a small investor with limited experience who invests in individual stocks and plays the market. Everybody knows someone down the block or in the next apartment who dabbles in the market and consistently (at least, so he says) makes money. Resist the temptation to do it yourself, or to let your friend invest it for you. The best and safest way to seriously invest in the stock market for your purposes is to find a well-managed fund and let the fund's management professionals do their job. Once you are satisfied with your selection, make your investment, continue to add to it every paycheck, and forget about day-to-day

---

[†] *This is not to be interpreted as advocating uncharitable attitudes. As human beings, we are our brother's and sister's keepers, not to mention the environment, politics, and all the other worthwhile efforts made to collectively help our society and the world we inhabit. But before you can afford the luxury of charitable giving, something we all should be obliged to do by our collective consciences, we must first be sure that we are secure ourselves, at least reasonably so.*

monitoring. It will seem to grow faster if you don't aggravate yourself about it every day or two.

If you're young and just starting out, your emphasis should be on long-term growth. Your investment strategy should be to find one or two good funds, invest regularly, and don't watch the stock. If you're halfway through your career or on the road to retirement, you'll need a fund that produces income or a combination of growth and income that you can adjust when you start to make regular withdrawals. Automatic payroll deduction is the best way to invest regularly for most of us, so we don't even have to think about it. Most employers can set this up for you. Don't even think of the money set aside for the fund as part of your salary. As far as you are concerned, your salary is what's left after each paycheck's deduction for the mutual fund has been made. If you can live on your base salary, then with a little thought and a bit of sacrifice you can live on ten percent less. Money invested thus will grow at least twice as fast as money invested in bank certificates of deposits at today's rates.

When you invest the same amount of money, month in, month out, a phenomenon called stock averaging kicks in. Here's how it works: If you invest, say, $500 in the Acme Stock Fund whose shares are selling for $50 per share, you get ten shares. If the share price goes to $100 per share and you still invest the same $500 each month, you are purchasing only five shares per month at the higher rate. On the other hand, if the price of the shares goes down, say, to $25 per share, the same $500 gets you twenty shares. You thus accumulate more shares at bargain prices and fewer shares at high prices, a shrewd investment philosophy that works for you on automatic pilot over a period of time.

Set Investment Goals

At first your financial goals should be modest. You need enough money so that you can afford to be out of work for one month, then two, then six, and finally for one year. As your nest egg grows you move your goal posts farther apart, and your goals become larger. It won't take as long as you think, and soon you'll have enough money saved to survive for two years without a job! It's not just the money you put away but also the growth of the fund (it's an aggressive stock fund, remember?) and the interest and dividends that kick in that will supercharge your modest in-vestments and soon have your financial motor purring along the road to financial security. When you have enough money to survive for one year, a wonderful thing happens. You suddenly realize that your fear of being fired has begun to recede. As long as you're working for a salary the fear will be there, especially if you have been fired before, but when you can survive for one or two years, your brain and your heart will tell you it's okay to relax a bit. That is the point when being fired recedes as a potentially ruinous disaster.

Putting the Financial Capstone in Place

Let's say that you earn $40,000 per year as a programmer at Billingsgate Electronics. If you can save fifteen percent of that you'll bank $6,000 a year, before taxes. At that rate you will have saved $30,000 or so in five years. If you figure in the compounding of ongoing contributions to savings, it will be more in the range of $40,000. That's enough to support yourself for a full year. But by that time, figuring in raises and bonuses, you should be earning more than your starting salary five years ago. In order to make sense of your efforts to save, you need to set goals, so you know where you're going and approximately how long it will take.

With enough money to live on for two years you're ready to put the capstone of permanent, lifelong financial security in place. When this final goal is reached, you will never have to work for the rest of your life unless you choose to. You can decide to retire and spend your time on the beach, write the novel you've been thinking about, get the camper out and go on the trip of a lifetime, or live out whatever your fantasy is. You won't be a multimillionaire, but you will be financially secure, able to buy, within reason, whatever it takes to make you and your loved ones happy. Isn't that why we work? If you can get there while you're still young, isn't that worth some sacrifice? Even if you just want to end the fear of being fired again, that's enough of an accomplishment to make the effort worthwhile.

One caution: Don't let your pursuit of the dollar and financial security become the only goal in your life. Life is more than the accumulation of money, and if that's your only goal, you will live a shallow, unsatisfying, and ultimately unhappy life. The miser is a familiar figure in literature and life. We all know someone who never picks up the check, who is so bound up in insecurity that he becomes laughable in his miserly attitude, were he not so pitiful. The difference between a frugal person and a miser is a matter of degree. The miser is a misfit with emotional problems. Although his fortune may be enviable, his life is not. The murderous uncle in Robert Louis Stevenson's novel *Kidnapped*, or the darkly comical Ebenezer Scrooge in Dickens' *A Christmas Carol*, are two characters who embody the dark side of money mania. Don't let the pursuit of wealth warp your perceptions of life. Money is only a tool to help reach various goals and provide the necessities and a few luxuries. It's a perfect slave but a horrible master.*

How to Set Retirement Goals

Here's a rule of thumb to figure your financial retirement goals. For every $10,000 in interest income you want your investments to produce for you, you'll need around $120,000 in your fund. These are approximate figures because every situation is different. This example assumes an interest rate of eight to ten percent. Now, figure out the desired return needed to support your lifestyle and financial needs. Let us assume that the amount you need is $60,000 a year. To produce that sum you'll need an invested sum of about $720,000! Impossible? Not at all. Here's how:

- *Believe in Yourself and Your Future:* If you believe in yourself (and have a bit of luck in the bargain), your salary will increase over the years, plus you should get bonuses and other remuneration. Therefore, you should be able to increase your investment nest egg contributions accordingly, hastening your arrival at your goals.

- *Count Only Invested Income:* Consider the income streams and financial assistance to be provided by pensions, Medicare, Social Security, and other forms of income you may get as icing on the cake. Don't figure them into your equations. That way, if they come, great. If not, you'll still be okay.

- *Money Makes Money:* Here's a simple trick to figure out how long it will take your investment to double. Take the percentage rate of

---

H. L. Hunt, the Texas billionaire, was said to have gone to work each day with a brown paper bag containing his lunch. After he finished eating it (at his desk), he carefully refolded the wax paper sandwich wrap and put it into the bag, which he brought home at the end of the day for use the next day, until the paper eventually wore out. He wore the same shirt for one week, then had it laundered and wore it again the next week.

return you are getting on your investment and divide it into 72. The answer is the number of years it takes to double your money. Thus $40,000 invested in a fund that returns nine percent a year will double every eight years. Your hypothetical $40,000 will become $80,000 in eight years, $160,000 in sixteen years, $320,000 in twenty-four years, and $640,000 in thirty-two years. That's enough to retire on. But you need all that money before then. Who wants to wait thirty-two years?

You haven't stopped saving and adding to your base amount after you accumulated the initial $40,000. You will have doubtless gotten some raises and bonuses also and increased the amount you've been contributing to your fund accordingly. Every five years or so you'll feed another $40,000 into the pipeline, more if you increase the percentage of your income you are tithing, and still more if you can find a fund that safely returns better than our hypothetical nine percent. If you hold down a second or part-time job in addition to your regular job your savings will grow in the express lane. And if your spouse works and you bank his or her salary, you'll reach critical investment mass still sooner. I found a fund that returns 11 1/2 percent consistently. That means that my funds are doubling every six years or so. I am willing to take some risk for those kinds of returns. Are you? If not, you might consider spreading your risk over two or three different funds, with an aggressive fund, a middle-of-the-road fund, and a conservative fund. The real key is to invest the same amount at the same time each month in each fund.

Remember, your first goal is to finance yourself for one, then two years when not working. Once you've achieved these goals you can begin working on your long-range plan, outlined above. But your arrival at these first goals will give you a peace of mind and independence of spirit that will improve your feelings of self-esteem and relax your concerns, so that the quality of your life is immediately improved. Once you get the ball rolling, compounding interest, stock averaging, additions to the base amount from fresh money, and all the other things that happen once it all gets started enhance the overall picture. Before you get started, explore the IRA option and other plans available to shelter your funds while you're investing, against the time you will need to draw them out.

- *Don't Plunge or Gamble:* It's tempting to bet the ranch on a sure thing. Resist the temptation. Any financial opportunity that you are offered—and when word gets out that you have some money to invest, you'll find entrepreneurs beating a path to your door—that sound too good to be true . . . are too good to be true. Diversify if you feel insecure with all your money in one pot, but stay away from the high flyers. Unless you're already wealthy you can't afford to piddle away your modest stake on "sure thing" gambles. You may hit it one or two times but lose it all on the next one. If you have been to Las Vegas, you know the drill. Win a few bucks on the slots or blackjack, and you lose it all five minutes later. Yes, people do win the jackpot occasionally. But it takes hundreds of losers to give up their hard-earned money to finance a few winners. The only ones who really win are the casino owners. Slow and steady will get you there, sooner rather than later.

- *Invest in Real Estate:* After you reach your first or second goals, consider buying a condo or a house so you can get out of the rent trap. This will result in still more savings. You'll be able to shelter part of your interest income if you have a mortgage. In addition, by paying off the mortgage you are slowly creating another pot of money for later use. Your property should increase in value the longer you have it.

- *Don't Touch the Principal:* As you build a base of invested capital, regard that money as sacred, never again to be touched unless the direst of emergencies arises. Consider your base capital as the engine that powers your financial security. The bigger the engine the more powerful is your ability to do things with it, and the greater your security becomes—and sooner. If you want to buy a car, for example, save up enough interest income for a down payment or even the whole amount and make the payments, if any, from your monthly interest income and not by eating into capital. You'll never get anywhere if you use up your capital, no matter how worthy the cause. Wait until you have enough coming in each month, and if you must take money from yourself, take the interest in monthly dribbles.

- *When the Time Comes, Start Paying Yourself:* You'll eventually reach the point where your invested capital reaches "critical mass." Everyone defines that according to his or her individual plan. I consider critical mass to be around $100,000. That is a magical figure, the achievement of which permits you to consider taking some money out of the fund each month if you need it for any purpose. Just remember, though, that every dollar you take out of the fund and don't allow to be reinvested slows your arrival at your major goal accordingly. But there are times when you need to take money. Life goes on and is sometimes expensive. Ideally you'll never take funds until you reach your goal of complete financial independence or retirement. But life is never neat and tidy, and you will on occasion need money.

- When that time comes and you must take out funds, take out only what you absolutely need. Try to finance it over several months if you can, so that you take the money only from interest and not capital.

    Remember these three rules:

    1. Capital, once created can never be created again, only added to.

    2. The purpose of creating capital is to acquire enough to throw off sufficient interest to use.

    3. *Once it has been created, never touch your capital unless it's a matter of life and death.* If you make regular withdrawals, leave some interest in the fund to fight inflation and keep the fund growing.

Each time you reach another financial goal, it's party time. Take a few hundred dollars out of the fund and throw a party, or take your sweetheart on a vacation. Life is to be lived and money is to make it possible—and enjoyable. By always taking a little out for party time you'll maintain your link to reality and resist the temptation to make your financial goals so overwhelming that you become a slave to savings. Because you know that a nice reward awaits you at the end of each level you reach, you'll tend to stay with the plan until you can collect your reward.

Howard Hughes was one of the wealthiest men in the world, and one of the unhappiest. His mania for making money eventually unhinged him and he died a miserable, sick, and lonely man. While his tragedy is the stuff of Hollywood movies, it happens on smaller scales all the time to people you'll never hear about. Saving money can be hazardous to your health. Take care to safeguard your mental health by keeping savings in perspective. Take the time to smell the flowers as you stash away your future happiness.

THE QUOTERY

24

"Here may you find comfort and rest, here may you find life at its best," goes the quote from a popular sampler of the last century. You can rest after you achieve your goal of getting another job, but comfort is something we need constantly, especially during the period after the firing, when we are most vulnerable, confused, and frightened.

Remember, you are not alone in your experience with this terrible function of commercial life in America and elsewhere. Others have experienced the pain of rejection, the feelings of failure and worthlessness that burdened your heart in the hours following your firing.

Throughout the centuries, mankind has produced countless quotes, maxims, and sayings from the accumulated wisdom of experience. The quotes in this chapter were selected for their relevance to the experience of being fired. They're like comfortable old slippers. They shape themselves to our minds, "downsize" our weaknesses, and reinforce our strengths with their pithy insights. They are mini-prayers of enlightenment and healing. Park your bookmark in this section and refer to it frequently. Enter into "The Quotery" as you would a temple containing a well of wisdom built just for you and, to paraphrase Alexander Pope, drink deeply.

Change and growth take place when a person has risked himself and dares to become involved with experimenting with his own life.

—Herbert Otto

The beginning is the most important part of the work.

—Plato

This time, like all times, is a very good one, if we but know what to do with it.

—Emerson

Life shrinks or expands in proportion to one's courage.

—Anaïs Nin

Only those who will risk going too far can possibly find out how far one can go.

—T. S. Eliot

One comes to be of just such stuff as that on which the mind is set.

—The Upanishads

We have met the enemy, and he is us.

—Walt Kelly (from Pogo)

I think the person who takes a job in order to live—that is to say [just] for the money—has turned himself into a slave.

—Joseph Campbell

A craft can only have meaning when it serves a spiritual way.

—Titus Burkhardt

One company's fired person is another company's hired person.

—Robert Rintz

Nothing succeeds like failure.

—Eugen Weber

Failure is not something to be avoided. It's a natural and necessary part of life.

—Wayne Allen Root

Never fall in love with your job; it can't love you back.

—Peter Ueberroth

Your first responsibility is to yourself. Next comes your family. Then comes your job.

—Peter Ueberroth

Follow that will and that way which experience confirms to be your own.

—Carl Jung

To know oneself, one should assert oneself.

—Albert Camus

I must create a system or be enslaved by another man's.

—William Blake

If I do not think of myself, who will think of me? If I do not think of others, then what kind of man am I? If not now, when?

—The Talmud

But then, if I do not strive, who will?

—Chang Tzu

Don't listen to friends when the Friend inside you says, "Do this."

—Gandhi

One way or another, we all have to find what best fosters the flowering of our humanity in this contemporary life, and dedicate ourselves to that.

—Joseph Campbell

Everyone has been made for some particular work, and the desire for that work has been put in every heart.

—Rumi

Look within thine ears.

—Shakespeare

The vocation, whether it be that of the farmer or the architect, is a function; the exercise of this function as regards the man himself is the most indispensable means of spiritual development, as regards his relation to society [it is] the measure of his worth.

—Ananda K. Coomaraswamy

Consciously or unconsciously, every one of us does render some service or other. If we cultivate the habit of doing this service deliberately, our desire for service will steadily grow stronger, and will make, not only for our own happiness, but that of the world at large.

—Gandhi

The Perfect Way is only difficult for those who pick and choose; Do not like, do not dislike: all will then be clear.

—Seng-TS'An

You wish to see; listen. Hearing is a step toward vision.

—St. Bernard

The work will teach you how to do it.

—Estonian proverb

All labor that uplifts humanity has dignity and importance and should be undertaken with painstaking excellence.

—Martin Luther King, Jr.

A first-rate soup is more creative than a second-rate painting.

—Abraham Maslow

Whoever does not detach himself from the ego never attains the Absolute and never deciphers life.

—Constantin Brancusi

The will to be oneself is heroism.

—Ortega y Gassett

Life is either a daring adventure or it is nothing.

—Helen Keller

All the world is full of suffering, it is also full of overcoming it.

—Helen Keller

We are what we think. All that we are arises with our thoughts. With our thoughts we make the world.

—Buddha

You can't depend on your judgment when your imagination is out of focus.

—Mark Twain

Has fear ever held a man back from anything he really wanted, or a woman either?

—George Bernard Shaw

Let me not pray to be sheltered from dangers
but to be fearless in facing them.
Let me not beg for the stilling of my pain,
but for the heart to conquer it.

—Tagore

Those who reach greatness on earth reach it through concentration.

—The Upanishads

Courage is not the absence of fear, but rather the judgment that something else is more important than fear.

—Ambrose Redmoon

You can and you must expect suffering.

—Mother Teresa

The miracle is not that we do this work, but that we are happy to do it.

—Mother Teresa

There is nothing with which every man is so afraid as getting to know how enormously much he is capable of doing and becoming.

> —Sören Kierkegaard

One cannot always be a hero, but one can always be a [hu]man.

> —Goethe

Not I—not anyone else, can travel that road for you, you must travel it for yourself.

> —Walt Whitman

Man is not the creature of circumstances. Circumstances are the creatures of men.

> —Benjamin Disraeli

Nurture your mind with great thoughts. To believe in the heroic makes heroes.

> —Benjamin Disraeli

Seek and ye shall find.

> —Luke 11:9

Human beings can alter their lives by altering their attitudes of mind.

> —William James

Compared to what we ought to be, we are half awake.

> —William James

Man is unhappy because he doesn't know he's happy.. . . If anyone finds out he'll become happy at once.

> —Dostoyevsky

Successful people are the ones who turn dreams into reality. The rest of us do the opposite.

> —Jeff Macnelly, "Shoe," *Los Angeles Times*, June 26, 1996

Keep away from people who try to belittle your ambitions. Small people always do that, but the really great make you feel that you, too, can become great.

> —Mark Twain

It is the first of all problems for a man [or woman] to find out what kind of work he [or she] is to do in this universe.

—Thomas Carlyle

Don't listen to what they say. Go see.

—Chinese proverb

It is our duty as men and women to proceed as though the limits of our abilities do not exist.

—Pierre Teilhard de Chardin

Alas! The fearful unbelief is unbelief in yourself.

—Thomas Carlyle

You must be the change you wish to see in the world.

—Gandhi

No one knows what he can do until he tries.

—Publilius Syrus

Man is what he believes.

—Chekhov

You see things and say, "why?" but I dream things that never were and say, "Why not?"

—George Bernard Shaw

Why not spend some time determining what is right for us, and then go after that?

—William Ross

We are prone to judge success by the index of our salaries or the size of our automobiles rather than by the quality of our service and relationship to mankind.

—Martin Luther King, Jr.

Work to become, not to acquire.

—Elbert Hubbard

Few men ever drop dead from overwork, but many quietly curl up and die because of undersatisfaction.

—Sidney J. Harris

It is the chiefest point of happiness that a man is willing to be what he is.

—Desiderius Erasmus

All the world's a stage, and all the men and women merely players.

—Shakespeare

I will act as if what I do makes a difference.

—William James

Live your life as though every act were to become a universal law.

—Henry David Thoreau

Your work is to discover your work and then, with all your heart, to give yourself to it.

—Buddha

Here is the test to find whether your mission on earth is finished: If you're alive, it isn't.

—Richard Bach

In the long run you hit only what you aim at. Therefore, though you should fail immediately, you had better aim at something high.

—Henry David Thoreau

If people knew how hard I worked to get my mastery, it wouldn't seem so wonderful after all.

—Michelangelo

It is your work in life that is the ultimate seduction.

—Pablo Picasso

He did his best with what he had.

—Justice Thurgood Marshall (when asked how he wanted to be remembered)

Do what you can with what you have, where you are.

—Theodore Roosevelt

We know what we are, not what we may become.

—Shakespeare

We never know how high we are
Til we are called to rise.
And then, if we are true to plan
Our statures touch the skies.

—Emily Dickinson

Man's capacities have never been measured, nor are we to judge of
what he can do by any precedent, so little has been tried.

—Henry David Thoreau

[One] who is naturally and constitutionally adapted to and trained in
some one or another kind of making, even though he earns his living
by this making, is really doing what he likes most, and if he is forced
by circumstances to do some other kind of work, even though more
highly paid, is actually unhappy.

—Ananda K. Coomaraswamy

It sometimes seems that intense desire creates not only its own oppor-
tunities, but its own talents.

—Eric Hoffer

A life mission is not simply an occupation. Rather, it's a steady appli-
cation of effort to the lifelong challenge of remaining true to your best.
It's the love of your life in action.

—Laurence G. Boldt

If you only care enough for a result, you will almost certainly attain it.

—William James

Our plans miscarry because they have no aim. When a man
does not know what harbor he is making for, no wind is the
right wind.

—Seneca

Do not turn back when you are just at the goal.

> —Syrus

Nothing is as exhilarating as being fired at with real bullets and being missed.

> —Winston Churchill

I believe that anyone can conquer fear by doing the things he fears to do.

> —Eleanor Rossevelt

The only thing we have to fear, is fear itself.

> —Franklin Roosevelt

The greater part of all the mischief in the world arises from the fact that men do not sufficiently understand their own aims.

> —Goethe

I have learned this at least by my experiment: that if one advances confidently in the direction of his dreams, and endeavors to live the life which he has imagined, he will meet with success unexpected in common hours.

> —Henry David Thoreau

Our aspirations are our possibilities.

> —Robert Browning

Always bear in mind that your own resolution to succeed is more important than any other one thing.

> —Abraham Lincoln

Without work, all life goes rotten. But when work is souless, life stifles and dies.

> —Albert Camus

He conquers who endures.

> —Persius

You are what you do.

> —Anonymous

Trifles make perfection, and perfection is no trifle.

 —Michelangelo

Obstacles will look large or small to you according to whether you are large or small.

 —Oswald Swett Marden

A strong passion . . . will insure success, for the desire of the end will point out the means.

 —William Hazlitt

I guess it never hurts to hurt sometimes.

 —The Oak Ridge Boys

Take this job and shove it.

 —Johnny Paycheck

You can knock me to my knees, but you cannot make me crawl while I'm down there.

 —Jeannie Seely

The surest way to get fired from your job is to tell the truth consistently.

 —Murray Vidockler

If you're wired, you're fired.

 —Willie Nelson

Desire creates the power.

 —Raymond Hollingwell

Wisdom begins with sacrifice of immediate pleasures for long-range purposes.

 —Louis Finkelstein

I didn't like picking cotton one bit. I used to stand in the fields and watch the cars go by and think, "I want to go with them."

 —Willie Nelson

Nothing is more difficult, and therefore more precious, than to be able to decide.

> —Napolean I

Choose always the way that seems the best, however rough it may be. Custom will soon render it easy and agreeable.

> —Pythagoras

Everybody lives by selling something.

> —Robert Louis Stevenson

Nothing happens in life until someone sells something to someone else.

> —Anonymous

Only a life lived for others is a life worthwhile.

> —Albert Einstein

Revenge is a dish best eaten cold.

> —Anonymous

They conquer who believe they can.

> —Ralph Waldo Emerson

You must push yourself beyond your limits, all the time.

> —Carlos Casteneda (Don Juan)

My wife said to me: "You're always trying to get something for nothing! Don't you realize that hard work never hurt anybody?" I said, "Yeah, I realize that, and I don't want to take any chances on spoiling its record!"

> —The Duke of Paducah

Whether you think you can or you can't—you are right.

> —Henry Ford

I feel like shit.

> —Lee Iacocca, upon being fired

Take time to deliberate; but when the time for action arrives, stop thinking and go in.

—Andrew Jackson

Nothing clears the mind so wonderfully as the sight of a noose.

—Samuel Johnson

This ole gal used to think happiness resulted when my earnings matched my yearnings.

—Patsy Cline

Nothing succeeds like the appearance of success.

—Christopher Lasch

You're a solo artist in this band, so you might as well really be a solo artist.

—Eddie Van Halen (parting words as he fired singer Sammy Hagar)

Blessed is he who has found his work. Let him ask no other blessing.

—Thomas Carlyle

A wise man will make more opportunities than he finds.

—Francis Bacon

To climb steep hills requires slow pace at first.

—Shakespeare

The best thing you can do for the poor is not to be one of them.

—Merle Haggard

They say a mind is a terrible thing to waste. Well, I say a dream is a terrible thing to waste.

—Dolly Parton

If you want the rainbow, you gotta put up with the rain.

—Dolly Parton

The people who get on in this world are the people who get up and look for the circumstances they want, and, if they can't find them, make them.

—George Bernard Shaw

It is one of life's laws that as soon as one door closes, another opens. But the tragedy is that we look at the closed door and disregard the open one.

—André Gide

Success is about having to worry about every damned thing in the world except money.

—Johnny Cash

Notes

Chapter 1

1. Thomas I. Palley, "The Forces Making for an Economic Collapse," *The Atlantic Monthly*, July 1996, 44.

Chapter 4

1. Lee Iacocca, with William Novak, *IACOCCA, An Autobiography*, (New York: Bantam Books, 1984).
2. *Los Angeles Times*, July 31, 1996, A8.
3. *Los Angeles Times*, July 27, 1996, D1.
4. *Los Angeles Times*, article by Henry Weinstein, April 25, 1996, A16.

Chapter 5

1. Alan Downs, *Corporate Executions* (New York: Amacom, 1995), 22.
2. John Greenwald, "Spinning Away," *Time*, August 26, 1996, 30.
3. Ibid.

Chapter 6

1. *Time*, July 8, 1996, 45.
2. Quoted in the *Chicago Tribune*, August 4, 1996.
3. "You're Fired—er, Hired!" *Time*, July 8, 1996.
4. Jack Beatty, "The Year of Talking Radically," *The Atlantic Monthly*, June 1996, 20.

Chapter 11

1. Taken from Kahlil Gibran's *The Prophet*, N.Y. Random House, 1968.
2. Quoted in Tom Jennings, "The King of Pain," *The Los Angeles Reader*, April 12, 1996, 3.

Chapter 12

1. "Terminated Employee Has Right to See Personnel File," *Los Angeles Times*, June 30, 1996, D16.

Chapter 13

1. Lindsey Novak, "At Work," *Chicago Tribune*, July 28, 1996.

Chapter 15

1. Kathleen A. Riehle, *What Smart People Do When Losing Their Jobs* (New York: John Wiley & Sons, 1991), 150.

Chapter 16

1. William J. Morin and James C. Cabrera, *Parting Company* (New York: Harcourt Brace, 1991), 243.

Chapter 17

1. U.S. Bureau of Labor Statistics bulletin no. 2472, *Employment Outlook, 1994–2005: Job Quality and Other Aspects of Projected Employment Growth* (Washington, D.C.). Recommended reading for job seekers.
2. "The American Dream, In Technicollar," *Los Angeles Times*, September 1, 1996, M5.
3. Ibid.

Chapter 18

1. *Los Angeles Times,* June 24, 1996, Business section, part II, 13.

2. Ibid.

Chapter 23

1. Vicki Torres, "Ruling Protects Franchise Owners from Abusive Chain Practices," *Los Angeles Times,* August 15, 1996, D1.

BIBLIOGRAPHY

Beck, Ross R., Ph.D., and Brian G. Long, Ph.D. *The Win-Win Negotiator.* New York: Pocket Books, 1987. $7.95, paper, 108 pp.

Brown, Mara. *Landing on Your Feet.* Whitby, Ont.: McGraw Hill Ryerson, 1992. $14.95, paper, 284 pp.

Byron, William J., S.J. *Finding Work Without Losing Heart.* Holbrook, Mass.: Adams Publishing Co., 1995. $12.95, hardcover, 224 pp.

Dixon, Pam, and Sylvia Tiersten. *Be Your Own Headhunter Online.* New York: Random House, 1995. $16.00, paper, 394 pp.

Downs, Alan. *Corporate Executions.* New York, American Management Association, Amacom, 1995. $22.95, hardcover, 225 pp.

Elderkin, Kenton W. *How to Get Interviews from Classified Job Ads.* New York: Wing Books, 1993. $11.99, hardcover, 230 pp.

Kirkwood, Christopher. *Your Services Are No Longer Required.* New York: Penguin, New American Library, 1993. $9.00, paper, 212 pp.

Morin, William J., and James C. Cabrera. San Diego: Harcourt Brace, 1991. $9.95, paper, 386 pp.

Petras, Kathryn, and Ross Petras. *The Only Job Hunting Guide You'll Ever Need.* New York: Simon & Schuster, Fireside, 1995. $15.00, paper, 398 pp.

Quittel, Frances. *Fire Power.* Berkeley: Ten Speed Press, 1994. $11.95, paper, 240 pp.

Richardson, Douglas B. *National Business Employment Weekly's "Networking."* New York: John Wiley & Sons, 1994. $10.95, paper, 200 pp.

Riehle, Kathleen A. *What Smart People Do When Losing Their Jobs.* New York: John Wiley & Sons, 1991. $10.95, paper, 180 pp.

Smith, Holly S. *How to Bounce Back After Losing Your Job.* Chicago: VGM Career Horizons, 1993. $12.95, paper, 116 pp.

Thompson, John A., with Catherine A. Henningsen. *The Portable Executive.* New York: Simon & Schuster, Fireside, 1995. $12.00, paper, 267 pp.

X, Mr. *Fired? Fight Back!* New York: American Management Association, Amacom, 1995. $16.95, paper, 194 pp.

Yate, Martin. *Knock 'Em Dead.* Holbrook, Mass.: Adams Publishing Co., 1995. $10.95, paper, 300 pp.